Navigating the Sermon

Lent and Easter Seasons Edition for Cycle A
of the Revised Common Lectionary

A Compilation of "Charting the Course" Columns from
Emphasis: A Preaching Journal for the Parish Pastor
a Component of **SermonSuite.com**

CSS Publishing Company, Inc.
Lima, Ohio

NAVIGATING THE SERMON
LENT AND EASTER SEASONS EDITION, CYCLE A

FIRST EDITION
Copyright © 2013
by CSS Publishing Co., Inc.

Most scripture quotations are from the New Revised Standard Version (NRSV) of the Bible. Copyright 1989 by the Division of Christian Education of the National Council of the Churches of Christ in the USA. Used by permission.

Scripture quotations marked RSV are from the Revised Standard Version of the Bible, copyrighted 1946, 1952 ©, 1971, 1973, by the Division of Christian Education of the National Council of the Churches of Christ in the USA. Used by permission.

Scripture quotations marked TEV are from the Good News Bible, in Today's English Version. Copyright © American Bible Society 1966, 1971, 1976. Used by permission.

Scripture quotations marked NIV are taken from Holy Bible, New International Version, copyright © 1973, 1978, 1984 International Bible Society. Used by permission of Zondervan Bible Publishers. All rights reserved.

For more information about CSS Publishing Company resources, visit our website at www. csspub.com, email us at csr@csspub.com, or call (800) 241-4056.

ISBN-13: 978-0-7880-2744-4
ISBN-10: 0-7880-2744-1   PRINTED IN USA

Table of Contents

Introduction   5

Ash Wednesday   7
Called to a different life by Mark Molldrem

Lent 1   11
The day God got lonely by Wayne Brouwer

Lent 2   16
Far from the tree by David Kalas

Lent 3   21
The jar left behind by William Shepherd

Lent 4   26
Believing is seeing by Wayne Brouwer

Lent 5   30
No spring chicken by David Kalas

Passion / Palm Sunday (Lent 6)   35
The wrong anthem by William Shepherd

Maundy Thursday   40
Long table by David Kalas

Good Friday   45
Why did Jesus have to die? by Wayne Brouwer

Easter Sunday   50
Breaking boxes by Wayne Brouwer

Easter 2   55
Now it's time to preach by David Kalas

Easter 3   60
Read the manual by William Shepherd

Easter 4   65
Finding safety in the call of the wild by Wayne Brouwer

Easter 5   70
Between acts by David Kalas

Easter 6   75
Our known God by David Kalas

Ascension of Our Lord   80
Ground rules by R. Craig MacCreary

Easter 7   85
Invisible link by Wayne Brouwer

About the Authors   91

Introduction

Over forty years ago, CSS Publishing Company was founded by two pastors and a Sunday school superintendent who had a vision to assist pastors "on the front lines" in their efforts to share the gospel of Jesus with people over the entire United States. The lectionary was taking hold over the country in an effort to bring a common message to people, no matter where they worshiped.

Over the years, CSS has published many different products. Of the more than 1,700 publications that have been produced in the history of the company, *Emphasis: A Lectionary Preaching Journal* has been one of the most popular. In its history, thousands of pastors and their congregations have benefited from the commentaries and insights found within its pages.

Navigating the Sermon is a collection of commentaries from "Charting the Course," which is at the core of what **Emphasis** is about. For each Sunday in the Cycle A lectionary, the writers who contributed to these columns have provided thematic guidance drawing together the lessons for each Sunday in the church year. Not only have they provided one idea for each Sunday, but most days have multiple themes from which to choose.

We are excited to offer this new resource to the readers of **Emphasis**, both old and new, and pray that this book will be a blessing to you and an invaluable aid to your preaching ministry.

The editors of CSS Publishing Company

Ash Wednesday
Joel 2:1-2, 12-17
2 Corinthians 5:20b—6:10
Matthew 6:1-6, 16-21
by Mark Molldrem

Called to a different life

The summer of 2000 was a devastating one for the western United States. Wildfires broke out in almost every state. Montana was declared a disaster area. The landscape was changed and will be different now and for generations to come. Grey smoke covered the horizon and ashes covered the earth.

We enter the season of Lent on Ash Wednesday, when ashes symbolically cover our lives with the sign of a sooty cross made upon our forehead. Lent, a forty-day preparation for Easter, helps us reflect upon our need for repentance and discipline in our lives. Any one day of the year we live our lives will give us grist to chew on for forty days, as we consider our relationship with God and with other human beings. Any one of us has enough sin in us to go around for everyone, amplifying the need for all of us to take seriously this opportunity to examine ourselves in light of the Law and the Gospel. Whatever we personally discover can be carried sorrowfully, yet expectantly, to the cross of Christ and offered for burial with him so that a new self can rise with him and live before him daily in a manner worthy of the gospel.

Joel 2:1-2, 12-17

Whose son are you? Joel was son of Pethuel. As such he could have been spokesperson of the family heritage or the family vision of itself for the future. Instead, Joel, gifted with words, surrendered his mouthpiece to Yahweh. Joel's name means "Yahweh is God." Joel became the spokesperson for God. He reminded the people of their heritage with Yahweh and of Yahweh's vision for his people. The people of Judah were his audience. The context was a locust plague described as God's army (2:11) bringing judgment upon the people for their sins. This plague was also a presage of other armies to come, notably the Assyrian hordes that would wreak their own blackness upon the mountains of both northern and southern kingdoms. Then would come the invasion of the Babylonian army, like waves of devastation one after another, like locusts — the cutting, swarming, hopping, destroying locusts (1:4).

At the heart of Joel's message of judgment, however, is the invitation to repent. Turn from sin and turn toward God, who, though capable of judging his people, "is gracious and merciful, slow to anger, and abounding in steadfast love" (2:13). *The Lutheran Book of Worship* (ELCA) uses these very words in its liturgy during Lent as a musical response of the people to the reading of scripture. The call to repentance is expressed with such exhortations as "awake... lament... be confounded... call... gather... cry" (1:5-14). Whereas some prophets use the expression, "Thus says the Lord," to garner attention, Joel scripts the blowing of the trumpet (2:1, 15). The people are to give heed to what is happening. The first blasting of the trumpet makes the people mindful that the day of judgment is coming. As much as one would like any day of reckoning to be far off, God's day "is near" (2:1). The second blasting of the trumpet draws the people's regard to the discipline of fasting. This can be an outward sign of an inner transformation of heart, as one comes before the heavenly judge with the paltriness of one's earthly efforts.

When Joel speaks of the coming day of the Lord as near, the question can be asked if there is time to repent. In one sense, the answer is no. The judgment is coming. It has been unleashed. That cannot be changed at this level of engagement. In another sense, the answer is yes! There is always time for repentance because this is the purpose for the judgment. The judgment is, in this regard, open-ended. It is not final. With the appropriate response of repentance — which is the purpose of the judgment in the first place — there are opened up all sorts of possibilities for God to work out the divine plan of salvation.

The image of rending the heart and not garments (2:13) defines the experience of repentance as necessarily an inner transformation, not necessarily an occasion for outward show. True change of behavior originates in a change of attitude, which comes from the heart. It is like when Jesus said that the good tree produces the good fruit, not the other way around (Matthew 7:17-20).

It is with the prophets' sense of judgment and their uncanny way of reaffirming the goodness of God in the midst of all evil that we enter into the Lenten season once again. We can accept the ashes on our heads as a temporal sign of our sorrow for sin and the acceptance of the judgment that must fall upon us as outcasts from Eden.

2 Corinthians 5:20b—6:10

The Corinthian church was a divided church. There were severe differences within the Christian community regarding worship practices (e.g., tongues), personal behavior (e.g., sexuality), public witness (e.g., lawsuits), and leadership (e.g., jealous sectarianism). That's a lot of conflict happening in just one place! Paul attempts to address these problems in his correspondence. It is doubtful that he was very successful in improving the situation in Corinth. He ends his first letter with a plea for the Lord to come (1 Corinthians 16:22)! That's like saying, "Let's get the boss down here on the line to square this mess!" His second letter ends with a straightforward plea/command, "Mend your ways, heed my appeal..." (2 Corinthians 13:11). If Paul could have written a later letter in the spirit of Philippians, we may be able to see Corinth in a better light. But no such letter seems to be forthcoming. Perhaps it is the stark contrast between Corinth and Philippi that enables Paul to express his heart so tenderly to his Christian friends to the north.

Arguably, the two key words in this text are *kataggassw* (reconcile) and *diakonoz* (servant, as in waiting on tables). The plea for reconciliation is his main thrust and part of his plea is based upon the personal example of his servanthood. (The portion of the letter prior to this lectionary text bases his plea for reconciliation on theological ground: the Corinthians are to be newly shaped by Christ in them and they are to recognize Paul's reconciling mediation as modeled after Christ's reconciling work between God and humanity.)

Paul demonstrates great patience and perseverance in his attempts to bring the Corinthian congregation to a state of reconciliation. He could have considered them as a whole as *anathema* (*anaqema*, accursed, 1 Corinthians 16:22), for which he opens the door at the end of his first letter. But he draws up short on that and continues to appeal to them so that they may yet have opportunity to "clean up their act."

The theological motivation for this to happen is what Christ did for us. In verse 21, Paul describes what Martin Luther would call "The Happy Exchange." Christ Jesus, the one who was sinless, takes our sin (rebellion against God manifested through contention with one another) upon himself and imputes to us his righteousness with which we can stand before God forgiven and accepted. This experience and the remembrance of it should provide a kind of template on which we can perceive our human relationships and model them in like manner. Paul uses the image of imitation in his correspondence with Corinth (1 Corinthians 4:16; 11:1) and also with other congregations (Ephesians 5:1; Philippians 3:17). The imitation is ultimately of God's love as demonstrated through Jesus. Much later, *The Imitation of Christ* (associated with Thomas à Kempis, 1380-1471, and the Brethren of the Common Life) would be written, describing how the Christian life is an imitation of Christ, helping Christians of many other congregations for centuries thereafter to come to terms with this noble calling of walking in the steps of Jesus.

When juxtaposed to Joel, one might say that the Day of the Lord is the Day of Jesus, thereby defining the coming judgment and the present mercy experienced in the work of Christ upon the cross. The locust plague has become the Lord's pain, whereby humanity's sin is placed on him, so that salvation can be given to us. We would accept the grace of God in vain were we not to let it shape our lives and pervade every pore of our being and direct us in all our relationships.

Paul adds another weight to his appeal, hoping to tip the balance in favor of more appropriate behavior from the Corinthians. He lifts up his own servanthood. It is important to note that he does not use the word *douloz* (slave), which has sometimes been translated "servant" (e.g., Romans 1:1; Galatians 1:10 RSV). When Paul describes his relationship with Christ, he uses that term to describe his abject submission to Jesus' ownership of his heart and soul. In describing his relationship with fellow Christians, specifically the Corinthians, he uses the image of waiting on tables. He is offering all that he has gone through as evidence that his ministry is authentic and he is worthy of being listened to when it comes to the practical matters of getting along and of witnessing faithfully to the gospel. He does not hold anything back. Amazingly, this does not come across as pompous boasting, but as a humble ledger, crediting Paul the *walk* to back up his *talk*.

Matthew 6:1-6, 16-21

Jesus is on a roll! Unfortunately for his hearers, he is rolling right over them. He is striking right to the misshapened heart of piety that misses the mark of purity. Centuries later, Saint Augustine would correctly observe that sin is basically turning in upon oneself. Here, Jesus applies the practical consequences of this when it comes to alms, prayer, and fasting.

In three tightly packed paragraphs, Jesus treats three primary examples of the spiritually disciplined life. In keeping with the prophetic tradition, as well as being consistent with other religious traditions at their best, Jesus identifies alms-giving, prayer, and fasting as worthy practices of piety. There is a delightful rhythm to these passages, which any preacher or public speaker should note well.

What is interesting to note about the content of Jesus' words is that he does not describe the *what* of piety, but the *how* of it. That is to say, Jesus does not prescribe how much alms one is to give, what exact words one should pray (Matthew's redaction in 6:7-15 needs to be taken into account here), or even what constitutes a fast. Jesus focuses on the heart of the pious one. What is motivating the righteous activity? Is it truly and purely an action offered for God and as an expression of one's devotion? Or is it performed for the public so that others may see just how religious and virtuous one is? For these acts to have spiritual impact, they are to be directed toward God.

With a twist of sarcasm, Jesus says that those who perform their religious activities so that others may see them and laud the doer have already received their reward. What is that reward? Human acclaim! We all know what that is worth. Hollywood speaks of everyone's desire to have fifteen minutes of fame. The world is willing to give that but then moves on quickly to other, more novel entertainments. Shakespeare described fame well when he wrote of every person being an actor "that struts and frets his hour upon the stage and then is heard no more" (*Macbeth*, Act V, scene v). In light of this, is it any wonder that Hamlet asks the existential question — "to be or not to be" (*Hamlet*, Act III, scene i)?

How much more satisfying to have the heavenly Father's eternal acclaim, his everlasting valuation! The pure in heart will seek only the joy of their maker as they give alms, pray, and fast. This can best be assured "in secret," where there is not the distraction of a public parade.

This is not to discredit totally temporal acknowledgment. As earthbound creatures, living in community, we need notable, public examples to emulate. This comes by hearing and seeing in the community square. What Jesus is driving at is the motivating factor and the reward sought. He wants his followers to realize that the true reward of pious activity is the deep, inner growth that develops in the relationship between the earthly believing child and the heavenly rewarding Father.

Application

We may have lost the trumpet as the public herald of tidings, but we still have our church bells. Would that they could be like Edgar Allen Poe describes them in "The Bells": "Brazen bells! What a tale of terror now their turbulency tells! ... How they clang, and clash, and roar!" But, alas, they are used only for chiming the hour or playing melodious hymns. The siren perched over city hall has replaced the church bells in sounding an alarm to the community — and, then, only with secular concern for safety of life and limb, not of soul. It remains for the trumpet voice of the preacher to ring with the truth of God's judgment and mercy for the world's soul in need of repentance.

With all the extensive bad publicity the church has received over sex scandals and money mismanagement, one has to wonder if the church has lost its moral authority to be heard by the world. The church itself needs to repent and return to righteous ground on which to stand. That ground is the scripture, on the one hand, and not the accumulated wisdom of the ages (secular humanism at its best), which is often passed off as gospel; on the other hand, that ground is also a public life worthy of the gospel. Christians need to understand clearly that our life together is not defined by a sense of good-feeling social fellowship nor good-doing social action. Our life together finds its source and center in God, who wields the weal and woe for all creation. Our life together stands, not on our work or lack thereof, but on the work of Christ for us. This is what we have to communicate clearly to the world, or we will be seen simply as but one element in a very complex social network of the human community hurdling through space on this particular speck of dust called earth, instead of the Body of Christ, the community of the covenant, that is to mentor the world to the living God.

This work can be taken up by individual congregations as they take a close look at themselves to identify where work needs to be done in order to mature in Christ-likeness. Neighboring congregations are at odds with one another. There is dissension within a congregation over worship practices, theology, or the acceptance of a new pastor. Misconduct suits are filed by parishioners against clergy or other staff. Unbecoming behavior is accepted too easily for the sake of retaining members. Corinth is alive in our own hearts and has come to roost in our pews. Congregations who dare to take an honest look at themselves will come to the conclusion that there are many things for which they need to repent as a group. The Christian witness to the community is at stake.

Just as the longest journey begins with the first step, so too the road to recovery for the church will begin with the actions individual Christians take in response to the gospel. Personal repentance can be likened to that first step. Although repentance itself is a complex movement of the spirit (involving conviction, contrition, confession, and correction), it can manifest itself by the simple acts of alms-giving, prayer, and fasting. Christians need to be encouraged in these ways so that they do not become lost arts of the religious life. There are already many reports documenting the poor giving habits of people, as we use most, if not all, of our money for "paying the bills" and "playing." Prayer becomes an exercise "at church" and "at mealtime" ("We even do it at McDonald's, Pastor!") but not the regular breath of the soul throughout every day, because we are so busy or distracted with other matters. Fasting becomes a foreign language in corpulent America, even while fitness fads of workouts and diets flash across the screen unendingly.

We can affirm the dignity of such spiritual disciplines, pointing out specifically the rewards that endure. The practitioner should not engage in these activities for public display or acclaim, but for the deeper, abiding rewards of peace and contentment and a growing relationship with the heavenly Father. Giving alms, praying, and fasting will also direct one into better choices in other various aspects of one's life, providing increased courage and wisdom to live righteously. There will also be increased humility, as one realizes there is so much more one could do for the Lord in these disciplines and in all areas of one's life. From humility comes a more gracious posturing in life, as one lives in relationship with others and the whole created order as a reflection of God's loving and merciful relationship with us all.

Perhaps then we will hear together "the rhyming and the chiming of the bells," replacing "the moaning and the groaning of the bells!"

The day God got lonely

Today is the first Sunday *during* Lent. This is an important fact to note. In Advent, Christmas, Easter, and Pentecost, the Sundays belong to the season. They are Sunday *of...* But during Lent, the Sundays are not part of Lent. The forty days of the season flow around the Sundays, calling us to share the journey of suffering with Jesus. The Sundays themselves, however, are islands of mercy, reminding us that Jesus is alive and forever victorious.

Still, the Sundays and the days of Lent cannot be separated, as the scripture passages for today remind us. Lent is about suffering, sadness, pain, and heartache. Mostly we focus on these things in the general life of humanity since the fall, and then concentrate them in the life of Jesus, particularly in the tough final weeks as he moved toward the cross. Yet the scripture passages for today remind us of another side of the suffering, sadness, pain, and heartache. It is the heart of God that aches and breaks, too, when we move away from our creational goodness.

Imagine the conversations among the Father, Son, and Spirit from all eternity. There are terms of endearment, songs of praise, and words of encouragement. Next imagine the creative energies that gave rise to this universe — the expression of the desires in the heart of God to spill out and spread lavishly the care and commitments and kindness that flow through the Trinity. This world, according to the Bible, is the grand outpouring of God's generous desire to multiply love and to enjoy creatures made in God's own image, having in themselves the ability to ever expand the joy of divine blessing.

The early days of creation must have been a marvelous time, both here on earth and in heaven above. The book of Job hints at the wonder when these words are found on the lips of God: "Where were you when I laid the earth's foundation... while the morning stars sang together and all the angels shouted for joy?" (Job 38:4-7 NIV). Imagine the amazement of creatures, mineral and animal, terrestrial and celestial, and physical and spiritual springing into being at the winsome song of God. Imagine all of these as the preparation for God's final creative work — shaping human life to be the reflection of the community of the Trinity! Suddenly the universe was alive with prayer, conversation, drama, and love. Suddenly there was music of oratory and tenderness of intimacy. Suddenly the house of divine manufacturing became a home of divine Spirit interconnected with human spirit.

Then we read of the disobedience in the Garden, and we feel the shuddering horror of humanities lost in sin. Later we encounter Jesus less than alone in the wilderness — "comforted" only by the devil. Out of these stories the impact of Lent takes a different turn; it is not only we humans who suffer and cry, who wander in death lands and cemeteries, who struggle to find meaning in an alien world. It is God, too, who is lonely. The loneliness of God is found in the Garden of Eden after Adam and Eve have left. No more daily walks and talks. No more teas or nectars. No more playful observations of the bounding impalas or the sneaky geckos. God is lonely.

When we walk with Paul down the family tree of humanity, we find the feud of the ages: Adam the First's kin on one side; Adam the Second's kin on the other. God is lonely again and Matthew reminds us that the loneliness of God takes on very human shape and pain when Jesus' own preparation for ministry was a forty-day tour of duty with only himself and the devil as companions. Feel the loneliness as these passages come alive today.

Genesis 2:15-17; 3:1-7

There are many ways to enter the book of Genesis and most of them are not easy. It seems that the world of Genesis is too far removed from our own. The creation stories do not answer many of the questions we want to ask of them. The people of the early chapters are almost cardboard cutouts with only one or two notable features each. The genealogies leave us wondering about their correlation with archaeological records.

One helpful way to listen to Genesis is through the ears of those at Mount Sinai in Exodus 20-24. While we may quibble about how the text of these early books of the Hebrew Bible came into being, there is no question that the story within the text indicates that the Bible began at Mount Sinai. Prior to the Exodus there was no written scripture. Abraham did not read a Bible. Jacob did not memorize Psalms. Joseph had no prophetic meditations to reflect upon while imprisoned in Egypt. Moreover, the Israelites forget who the God of their ancestors was during their multiple centuries of slave labor. Even Moses, who was specially saved and prepared by God for a work of leadership, did not know who this God was until Moses himself was about eighty years old! Only after the rushed exit from Egypt and the arduous trek through the wilderness did a number of things fall into place at Mount Sinai.

The covenant struck (or "cut," to be more accurate to the Hebrew) at Mount Sinai was shaped in the typical contract arrangements of the day. The Hittite nation had fashioned a standardized form of international treaty in something we today call the Suzerain-Vassal covenant. It usually had six parts: a *preamble* declaring the right of the sovereign to initiate the covenant relationship, a *historical prologue* explaining the background that produced this moment of covenant-making, the *stipulations* of the covenant relationship, *curses and blessings* that expressed outcomes to the covenant or its failure, a list of *witnesses* who would confirm the making of this covenant, and a *document clause* that told where the copies of the covenant would be kept and when they would be read. Interestingly, all six parts of this Suzerain-Vassal covenant structure are found in Exodus 20-24.

With that in mind, it appears that Genesis forms an extended historical prologue to the Sinai covenant, explaining in greater detail why this covenant has become necessary. Reading Genesis from that perspective begins to pull things into meaningful and preachable form. From the backward glance of the Sinai covenant-making event, Genesis falls into four story-cycles roughly encompassed by these chapters: 1-11, 12-25, 26-36, and 37-50. While every major story-cycle is composed of a number of shorter tales, there seems to be either a dominant character or an over-arching theme in each. Genesis 1-11 explain to the Israelites at Mount Sinai who God was (Creator) and the character of this God's creation (endowed with freedom, intended good, but now in a state of war with its Creator). Chapters 12-25 give Israel a sense of her special identity and how a covenant with God had shaped her from the very beginning. Chapters 26-36 answer the question of what kind of character Israel had based upon the stories of Jacob (the conniver) who became Israel (the one who wrestles with God). And chapters 37-50 tell how Israel came to live in Egypt.

In this light, the story of Adam and Eve in the Garden of Eden teaches Israel the nature of life (stewardship of the natural order), the desire of God (intimacy with humankind), and the limits of human conduct (freedom within the definable boundaries of God's commands). This is explained through the poetry of creation's birth (Genesis 1-2) and summarized in the first half of the Genesis text for today (Genesis 2:15-17).

The second half of today's text unfolds the beginnings of human rebellion. The origin of the serpent is not explained, nor is the serpent's unusual understanding of the human situation. Later, after the curse of Genesis 3:14-15, the serpent will effectively disappear from the narrative. In other words, the serpent functions here merely as a foil by which to process initial human transgression. Questions about the serpent cannot be answered from the text. The text is not about the serpent; it is about how humans became enemies of God. The text goes on to tell of the first sins — deliberate disobedience to a direct command of the Creator God — and then explains the outcome: alienation, separation, isolation, shame.

While the text for today cuts off the rest of the story, the outcome between Adam and Eve is the same as that between the humans and their God (3:8-24). Whatever intimacy there had been between God and these honored creatures is now gone. Adam and Eve lose communion with each other, and the human race begins its murderous slide. More importantly, God loses communion with Adam and Eve and both grow very lonely.

Romans 5:12-19

Paul was concluding his third mission journey (Acts 18:23—20:38) when he wrote this letter. He was wintering in Corinth at the time (Romans 16:23), staying with his good friend Gaius. Paul was on his way to Jerusalem to bring a financial offering for the poor in the Jerusalem church (Romans 15:26); he hoped soon afterward to make a personal visit to Rome (Romans 15:24-25). This letter anticipated Paul's coming and included a summary of his teachings.

In large outline, the first three chapters of Romans focus on the desperate plight of humankind, chapters 4-8 announce God's remedy through the work of Jesus, chapters 9-11 wrestle with the matter of Jewish election and Gentile participation in the plans of God, and the rest of the letter expresses ways in which Christian faith can be lived out in society. Here in chapter 5, Paul is summarizing the significance of Jesus' work. In the previous chapter Paul had pointed out that God must do what we cannot do; this was true even for Abraham. Although we cannot earn God's good pleasure, we are connected to it through faith and since the recent full revelation of God's plan in Jesus, the object of our faith is Jesus himself.

In the text for today, Paul sets next to one another two family trees. The first is the blighted and wilting horror growing from the misshapen stump of Adam (vv. 12-14). The second is the marvelous and vital sturdy living thing emerging from the trunk of Jesus Christ (vv. 15-17). All of us participate in the first by the accident of birth. As one wit put it, "Life is a sickness for which the only cure is death."

Theologians continue to debate whether this passage promotes ideas of universal salvation. The minimalist approach says no; we only transfer from one tree (Adam's) to the other (Christ's) when we actively believe in the sacrificial work of Jesus. The moderate version says maybe; we are all automatically transferred from Adam's family tree to Jesus' family tree, but those who choose again to challenge God and intentionally disobey will be sent back and perish when Adam's tree is burned. The maximalist understanding is that the grace and gift of God (see v. 15) exceed our ability to cling to any tree, and automatically places us in the family of Jesus. The call now is for us to live as if we honor that gift.

Whatever approach you take, the larger theme is clear: God was lonely when Adam's tree began to die outside the Garden of Eden, so God replanted a tree of human grace and glory and brought those whom God chose (some, many, or all of us) back into the family.

Matthew 4:1-11

Matthew's original audience was largely composed of Jewish Christians. Matthew's method of tying Jesus to the Old Testament heritage of Jewish faith involved demonstrating how Jesus relived the history of Israel in miniature, replaying the major events and eras of its formative period. Here Jesus mirrors the forty-year wilderness wandering of Israel in the Sinai desert by way of his own forty-day wilderness sojourn.

The three temptations that Jesus endures echo specific challenges Israel faced early in its national existence. Each of these incidents is reviewed by Moses in the early chapters of Deuteronomy. First, while traveling through the deserted wastelands of the wilderness, Israel had complained to God about lacking food and facing starvation (Exodus 16). Jesus encounters similar famishment and uses Moses' teaching in Deuteronomy 8 to resist a quick fix that would remove him from following Israel's path.

Second, Israel quarreled with Moses in Exodus 17:1-7, declaring to him that God's power was insufficient to care for their needs. Moses recalls this incident in Deuteronomy 6:16 and reminds the people that God has never failed them in the past. Because of this they ought not doubt or question God's ability to care for them in the future. When Jesus is placed by the tempter in a situation where God's care might be tested, Jesus quotes Moses' words (Deuteronomy 6:16) to resist such unnecessary exercises and stands his ground.

Third, immediately after these two incidents in Exodus 16-17, Israel faced the prospect of becoming lost among the other nations and reduced to being merely like them. The battle between Israel and Amalek in Exodus 17:8-16 was resolved only when Moses went up to "the top of the hill" (v. 9) and kept the national focus upward (Moses' hands needed to be lifted toward heaven) to Israel's true leader. The strength of Israel that day was not found in its military might but in its devotion to the God who transcended all national affairs. Similarly for Jesus, from a "high mountain" he is enabled to see the power and wealth of the nations, but only when he quotes Moses' reminder from Deuteronomy 6:13 can he resist the prospect of becoming merely a world leader. As with Israel, his mission is much greater.

Matthew clearly wants his readers to understand Jesus' forty days in the wilderness as parallel to Israel's forty years in the wilderness. In each case the messenger of God is tempted to give up or deny God's power or settle for a typically human resolution to a problem. Yet, as Matthew shows, Jesus mimics Israel's reliance on God and emerges from the wilderness experience with integrity intact and facing the next state of his mission with renewed confidence in God.

Two themes surface from this story of Jesus' wilderness temptations. First, there is the loneliness of God. It was the loneliness of God, following the expulsion of Adam and Eve from the Garden of Eden, which led God to seek other traveling companions. In Old Testament times, Abraham and his descendents were called to be God's tour partner. The wilderness experiences they went through together strengthened their dependence on one another, especially Israel's on God. In New Testament times Jesus replays Israel's existence and becomes the visible divine partner on earth. Jesus makes evident to those around him what it means to walk with God, even through wilderness times. In Jesus' steadfast commitments is found the example that others who wish to travel with God can follow.

Second, since Jesus is himself fully divine, his wilderness struggles allow God to experience life as an exile. Just as Adam and Eve were forced out of the Garden and into the "wilderness" apart from intimacy with God, so in Jesus God experiences the wilderness loneliness that humans have had to face these many centuries. It will be through this wilderness experience, leading right up to the loneliness of the cross, that Jesus endures the painful loneliness of humanity in its quest to return to the Garden and intimacy with God. Only when the words, "My God! My God! Why have you forsaken me?!" (Matthew 27:46; Mark 15:34) have been wrung from Jesus' heart on Golgotha will a solution to God's loneliness be found. That day God would rip apart the temple veil and emerge from God's isolation to return to human interaction once again. From that time forward the Spirit of God would come on the church and its people would again be the dwelling place of God.

Through the loneliness of Jesus is the remedy to the loneliness of both God and humanity finally found. So on this first Sunday during Lent we spend time on the island of grace that lifts us above the lonely forty-day walk of suffering and pain.

Application
Some years ago a woman wrote the following poem that she called "A Lonesome Middleager":

Do you know what it means to be lonely?
Do you know how it feels to be blue?
Do you know what it's like to feel
No one really cares just how things are with you?

Yes, it's nice to be friendly at church time;
You are thankful when they tell you they pray.
But what about long, lonely night hours,
Not to mention the following day?

You can call up your friends, and I do that;
You can ask them how they're doing, too.
But you wish that they'd say, "Come on over
And help us eat up the leftover stew."

Most everyone has a son or a daughter,
A husband, a mother, or sis.
But when you're alone with no loved ones,
To me, I just merely exist.

This woman has captured the painful power of loneliness. Charles Williams, when asked about the meaning of the Old Testament, said that it could be summarized as depicting "the loneliness of God." Dorothy Day gave this title to the story of her lifelong search for meaning and God, *The Long Loneliness*. In all of these we are reminded of the agonizing alienation that settles into our world when God and humanity are separated by sin (Genesis 3). Two family trees develop side by side (Romans 5), and Jesus walks through the wilderness experiencing both God's loneliness and also that of humanity (Matthew 4).

On this first Sunday during Lent, dig into the pain of alienation and let your people feel the angst of a world come undone by the separations of racism, social stratification, spiritual isolation, philosophic skepticism, and sinful inability to be ourselves or with others who matter. Then point to God's long quest to rejoin us, and God's desire to have us rejoin God in fellowship and show how each is powerfully portrayed in the wilderness walk of Jesus at the outset of this Lenten season.

Far from the tree

Two thousand years earlier, Abram sat alone one night, when the Lord came to speak to him. He had no children, but the Lord promised to make him into a great nation. His roots had grown deep into the Mesopotamian soil, but the Lord wanted to transplant him to Canaan. He had more years behind him than ahead of him, but the Lord's greatest plans for him were still yet to come.

Abram believed God, and Abram obeyed God. He trusted God's promises to him, though they were the height of improbability. And he went where God sent, though the apprehension and sacrifice involved are nearly inconceivable to most of us. The old hymn "Trust and Obey" could have been written by that ancient patriarch.

After 2,000 years, his descendants had numbered in the millions. His family tree was immense and his descendants were firmly established in and identified with the land where Abram himself was only and always an alien.

One of the descendants on Abram's family tree was Nicodemus. He was the sort of great-great-grandchild that a man of faith prays for. He was pious, knowledgeable, and a leader of his people. He was precisely the sort of descendant that should make Abram proud.

Two thousand years after Abram, Nicodemus came by night to speak to the Lord. He was full of questions and uncertainty. He had knowledge, to be sure, but little understanding. He had a manifested spiritual hunger, but he seems to have gone away unsatisfied. He reappears at the end, aiding in Jesus' burial, but it looks as if that he did not have the courage to do more than follow Jesus from a safe distance.

This particular apple, it seems, fell far from the tree.

Genesis 12:1-4a

The biblical author's style is terse. We are given no background information about Abram's relationship or contact with the Lord, we are offered no glimpse into the previous 75 years of Abram's life in his homeland, and we are provided with no details about Abram's decision-making process, his conversations with Sarah at this juncture, or the impetus for Lot accompanying him. All of these matters, where we would be glad for some elaboration, remain mysterious.

The Lord is not vague about the nature of the sacrifice he asks Abram to make. He itemizes what he asks Abram to leave behind: "your country and your kindred and your father's house" (v. 1). But the Lord is not equally clear about where Abram will go: "to the land that I will show you" (v. 1).

Could it be that this was Abram's first contact with the Lord? Poet Killian McDonnell imagines that it might have been: "Talk about imperious. / Without a 'may I presume?' / No previous contact, / no letter of introduction, / this unknown God / issues edicts. / This is not a conversation. / Am I a nobody / to receive decrees / from one whose name / I do not know?"

Of course, while we lament God's lack of specificity about Abram's destination, we face a different problem where God is specific. The Lord lays out for Abram his plans — big plans. The old man who has precisely no children will, in that new, strange land, become "a great nation" (v. 2). And though this anonymous Aramean is on the back nine of his life, God will make his name great. Even though he has, at present, no heir, he will have a heritage in which "all the families of the earth shall be blessed" (v. 3).

Perhaps it takes less faith to launch out into an unknown future than an improbable future. That was surely the sticking point in the majority report of Israel's search committee at the border of the promised land (Numbers 13:25-33), and so it is right that Paul should praise Abram for simply believing God.

Could it be that Abram's obedience was as quick a reflex as the text suggests? The Lord spoke to him and without fanfare or fuss Genesis simply reports, "So Abram went, as the Lord had told him" (v. 3). As we follow the story of Abram, we discover soon enough that he is not perfect. But here in this episode, he is surely a model of faithful obedience.

Again, McDonnell lends insight into Abram's mind: "In ten generations since the Flood / you have spoken to no one. / Now, like thunder on a clear day, / you give commands: / pull up my tent, / desert the graves of my ancestors, / leave Haran / for a country you do not name, / there to be a stranger.... / You come late, Lord, very late, / but my camels leave in the morning."

Romans 4:1-5, 13-17

Family lines and genealogies have always been big deals. They have been the source of bitter conflicts and dynastic wars in countries where it is essential to trace the royal line. They are the common-knowledge database in small towns and rural areas where everyone knows who was married to your grandpa's second-cousin. They are a source of pride for individuals who like to track their lineage back to a certain group of immigrants, to the American Revolution, or to the Pilgrims. They were important records in ancient Israel (much to the consternation of modern readers who get bogged down in the lists of who begat whom), and today we find that there are many emerging new resources for folks who are eager to trace their own family line as far as they can go.

Family lines were important to the Jews of New Testament times too. That's why the half-breed Samaritans were so despised. That's why Paul includes his lineage in his list of things he could boast about (Philippians 3:4-6). That's why John the Baptist and Jesus had to challenge the self-satisfied "children of Abraham" (Luke 3:7-8; John 8:31-41).

Paul presents to the Romans a new perspective on Abraham's family tree.

The distinction between the Jews and the Gentiles was an important one for the Jews. It may have been more or less of an issue for the Gentiles in different places, but faithful Jews everywhere made it an issue. Their law — or at least their prevailing understanding of it — required them to make it an issue.

That distinction naturally carried over into the early church, which was entirely Jewish at the beginning. As growing numbers of Gentiles came to Christ in the years following Pentecost, a genuine disagreement and debate rose up within the church. By what way can a Gentile come to Christ? To what extent does a Christian have to be a Jew?

The question sounds strange in our day. Most of our churches are probably 100% Gentile, and some of the people in our pews may never even have known a Jewish Christian. The controversy that was so heated within the early church, therefore, does not resonate much today.

We do understand at least this much, however, in most of our churches: when something has always been done a certain way, it's hard to change.

All of the early Christians had come to Christ by basically the same route and from the same point of departure. One can hardly blame them, therefore, for assuming that everyone needed to follow the same directions in order to arrive at the same destination. And those directions included the path of circumcision, with a right turn at the law, and regular stops at the Sabbath.

Paul looked at the Old Testament people of God, their covenants and their patriarchs, however, and he saw something else at work: faith.

Paul's argument takes several forms along the way, especially in his letters to the Romans and the Galatians. In this particular passage, the argument focuses on the example of Abraham, which is a powerful one. Abraham predates the law, and his "reckoned to him as righteousness" (v. 3) moment also predates his circumcision. That righteousness, Paul contends, was a function of Abraham's faith.

In the end, therefore, Paul is not trying to defend an additional way to salvation and to Christ; he's making a claim about the only way. The unquestioned assumptions about the law are false assumptions, for it is actually faith that puts us right with God and that is not a new thing, but rather that is the way it has always been. The real family line that traces a person back to Abraham, therefore, is not flesh and blood, but faith.

John 3:1-17

The chapter opens and we are introduced to a man named Nicodemus with three pieces of information: He was a Pharisee, a leader of the Jews, and he came to Jesus by night. None of those statements constitutes outright criticism of Nicodemus, but each one has an unfavorable connotation.

The word "Pharisee," of course, has acquired an entirely negative meaning for the people in our pews. That was probably not the prevailing connotation in Jesus' day, but the Pharisees are surely depicted in an unflattering way in the four gospels. We surmise that they are hypocrites in their living, superficial in their religiosity, blind to God's work in John the Baptist and in Jesus, and petty in both their legalism and their opposition to Jesus and his followers.

That Nicodemus was "a leader of the Jews" (v. 1) is also an uncomplimentary observation by John. The phrase "the Jews" appears sixty times in the gospel of John, and often they are characterized by either ignorance or antagonism toward Christ. To be one of their leaders, therefore, was not a favorable association.

Finally, that Nicodemus came to Jesus "by night" (v. 2) is not a small detail. Even if it seems insignificant to us as we read, the gospel writer insists on its significance sixteen chapters later when Nicodemus reappears and is identified as the one "who had at first come to Jesus by night" (John 19:39).

The significance of Nicodemus coming "by night" may be understood in the larger context of what "darkness" means in the fourth gospel. Darkness suggests confusion and uncertainty (12:35), the comfy refuge for evil (3:19), and the enemy of the light (1:5). In contrast to the darkness, Jesus identifies himself as the light (8:12), and thereby the antidote for both the darkness of the world and the darkness in which any individual soul lives. Finally, elsewhere, Jesus says to his arrestors that the night "is your hour, and the power of darkness" (Luke 22:53). The fact that Nicodemus came to Jesus "by night," therefore, is not a flattering detail. At best, it connotes confusion and bewilderment, and, at worst, it suggests something sinful and sinister.

The initial point of friction in Nicodemus' conversation with Jesus, of course, is over the matter of being "born from above" (v. 3). The original Greek phrase can be translated in several ways: hence the traditional "born again" in the KJV and "born anew" in the RSV. Jesus almost certainly spoke in Aramaic, and so the Greek adverb (*anothen*) in the text cannot be attributed directly to him. Nevertheless, the variety of possible meanings probably reveals the breadth of the truth involved.

That Nicodemus heard born "again" is evident in his response ("Can one enter a second time into the mother's womb and be born?" v. 4). That the birth is "anew," meanwhile, is consistent with other New Testament affirmations (such as 2 Corinthians 5:17; Colossians 3:9-10; 1 Peter 1:23). And that the new birth is "from above" is implicit in Jesus' later explanation that it means being "born of the Spirit."

From the start, Nicodemus is in over his head. He doesn't comprehend what Jesus is saying to him, and he's not on the same page with the spiritual truths Jesus is conveying. Illustrative of Nicodemus' confusion is the parallel use of the word "enter" in this passage. Nicodemus doubts that a person can enter a second time into the mother's womb, while Jesus declares that "no one can enter the kingdom of God without being born of water and Spirit" (v. 5). So Nicodemus' misunderstanding of this new birth has him looking back to the womb, while Jesus is pointing forward to the kingdom.

Jesus' reference to "being born of water" (v. 5) can be taken two ways.

On the one hand, the passage has often been cited as a reference to water baptism. There is nothing in the immediate context of the verse to suggest a baptism allusion, but other passages certainly juxtapose water and Spirit baptisms (such as Matthew 3:11; Mark 1:8; Luke 3:16; John 1:33; Acts 1:5, 11:16).

On the other hand, the "being born of water" phrase may be a reference to physical birth. We have observed that a woman's water breaks at the time of a baby's birth, and it may be that this is what Jesus had in mind. That interpretation would certainly fit as a response by Jesus to Nicodemus' reference to the womb in verse 4. Also, the distinction between physical birth and spiritual birth is clearly the theme of verse 6.

We see Nicodemus' arrival in this episode, but we never see his departure. For the first few lengths of the conversation, Nicodemus is hanging in there with Jesus, albeit struggling to understand. By verse 9, however, Nicodemus is stymied and far behind, and by the time the chapter ends he is no longer visible.

By the time our particular passage ends, Jesus has presented Nicodemus and us with three great truths to digest. The first is the aforementioned theme of being born again, anew and from above. The second is the nature and work of the Spirit, which Jesus uses a play on words with "wind" (v. 8 — both are *pneuma* in the Greek) to illustrate. And the third is the gospel truth of Jesus' own purpose and mission.

The final four verses of the lection offer three different insights into Jesus' mission. Verses 14-15 borrow from Israel's wilderness experience with the serpent on a pole (Numbers 21:1-9) to offer a picture of Christ on the cross. Verse 16, the classic gospel-in-a-verse, reveals God's motivation behind Christ's mission. This is of particular importance because it shows God's attitude toward "the world," which is another prevailing theme in John's gospel. The fourth gospel refers to "the world" or "this world" 71 times and it appears another twenty times in the five chapters of 1 John. Finally, verse 17 articulates God's saving purpose and merciful will. Ever since guilty Adam and Eve heard God coming in the Garden, human beings have expected that God was coming to condemn. We are profoundly surprised and relieved each time we realize that, no, he comes "in order that the world might be saved."

Application

The three lections for this week present us with two main characters: Abram and Nicodemus. They are a study in contrasts, and perhaps a side-by-side examination of the two men could instruct and challenge our congregations.

Abram appears in the Genesis and Romans passages, while Nicodemus is the key character in John 3. In the Genesis lection, Abram is notable for his quick and quiet obedience. In Paul's consideration of Abram's example in Romans, he focuses on Abram's faith. In John 3, meanwhile, Nicodemus appears in the shadows, uncertain and confused, and disappears again with hardly a trace.

Different people have come to different conclusions about Nicodemus. Some see his effort to speak up on behalf of Jesus (John 7:50-52) and his presence at Jesus' burial (John 19:39-40) as signs of his discipleship. Others regard these as weak efforts, half swings without follow-through, suggesting a man who remained basically timid and confused in his relationship to Jesus. John's gospel surely gives us a clearer endorsement of the Samaritan woman in chapter 4, and a more apparent redemption of Thomas (20:26-28) and of Peter (21:15-19).

Nicodemus reads a little like the third servant in the parable of the talents (Matthew 25:14-30). He certainly does not seem like a bad guy, an antagonist, or a villain, and yet, in the end, he seems to come up tragically short.

The irony is that he seems so promising at the beginning. He is pious, knowledgeable, and a leader among his people. He has the spiritual appetite to come to Jesus, the sense to initiate a meeting with him, and yet, in the end, we are left to wonder whatever became of him.

Abraham, by contrast, seems not at all promising. Sports fans like to debate, "If you could choose any player to build your franchise around, who would it be?" Well, if you were going to build a new nation, you wouldn't naturally choose a childless 75-year-old man. And you wouldn't plant him as a wanderer in a land already occupied by other peoples.

But the same God, who used a boy to defeat a giant and an undersized army to defeat the much larger Midianite force, also made a great nation out of Abraham. More than one, actually. We are not left to wonder whatever became of Abraham.

And so it seems that, in the providence of God, the real issue is not how promising a person is. God is the promising one in this relationship. The real issue is not how promising a person is, but how believing a person is.

An Alternative Application

Genesis 12:1-4a. We observed above that God was very clear with Abram about the details of where, what, and whom he would leave, but not nearly so clear about where he would go. Could it be that this is something of a pattern with God? Is it always the nature of his call on our lives that what we leave is explicit and what we gain is unknown?

This runs somewhat contrary to our nature, of course. When we make our plans, the destination is usually the first thing we determine. Which airport I fly out of, which airline I take, and where I have my layover — these are particulars about which I am flexible. But my destination — that is the given, the known.

God's itinerary for Abram, by contrast, was very detailed about his point of departure but the rest was rather vague.

Perhaps something of that uncertainty is captured in Jesus' words to Nicodemus when he compares the movement of the wind to "everyone who is born of the Spirit." If we are willing to allow the Spirit to fill our sails and guide our ship, we cannot predict where that wind will take us.

Perhaps Abram's own experience is embodied, too, in the calls to discipleship of Peter and Andrew (Matthew 4:18-20), James and John (Mark 1:19-20), Levi (Luke 5:27-28), and the several would-be disciples (Luke 9:59-62; 18:18-24). In every case, what they have to leave behind is rather obvious, while their future is unclear and unspecific.

Except that their future is with the Lord.

That was the key for Abram. That was the key for the disciples. And that is the key for us, too, in whatever call God has for us.

The jar left behind

I was reading the work of a well-known biblical critic who said, "Adequate water sources were crucial to migrant desert dwellers." Like it isn't for the rest of us?

Most of us do not have to search for oases, draw water by hand, or carry jugs back and forth. I still remember the television theme song of my hometown water company (although why a public monopoly needed commercials is beyond me):

> *Turn it on, and we'll come running.*
> *Turn it on, and we'll be there.*
> *Clean and bright, day and night,*
> *Indianapolis water comes running!*

Perhaps there were Hoosiers in the 1960s who could remember hauling their own water and would be grateful for indoor plumbing. Nowadays, city water companies sell their product in grocery stores. Not only do we take drinking water for granted, we are willing to pay extra to get it in designer bottles.

Not everyone is so lucky. As I write this, Florida residents are lining up for water in the wake of four (so far) hurricane strikes. They will not soon forget how much a jug of water weighs, something many in this world are quite familiar with. Our friends in Romania, Elena and Marjana, load up their plastic water jugs and drive into town to draw from the common well. It's a lot of work, even if you have a borrowed Volvo to bear the burden. But there is no running water at their house.

The biblical imagery of water is best understood once we get a grasp on the physics involved. Though the Romans had indoor plumbing, the Bible is largely shaped by a nomadic and rural culture in which water was both precious and a burden. You couldn't live without it, but you either had to live next to it or carry it. Weightlifting thus required no special equipment, only the basic necessities of life. And unless you lived next to it, the hike would get your aerobic training in as well.

The provision of water in the desert is the sign of God's presence according to the book of Exodus. The gospel of John takes the theme and pushes it further, casting Jesus himself in the role of the substance of life. Meanwhile, Paul's letter to the Romans states in plain language the function of Jesus in providing life to all.

Exodus 17:1-7

God sent Israel on a camping trip. It was outward bound, except the campers learned to trust not in themselves, but in the one who sent them on their way. As part of their training, Israel was taught to look to God for the most basic of needs, food (Exodus 16:1-36) and water (Exodus 15:22-27; 17:1-7). Their response would be a paradigm for their future life.

The wilderness stories (Exodus 15:22—18:27) trace the transition of Israel from Egypt to Sinai, from slaves to people whom God has instructed. Israel is on a journey somewhere between promise and fulfillment; the wilderness becomes symbolic of their progress in faith, which is slow at best. The standard

21

pattern in these stories (as in today's lection) is the complaint: The people are needy and they make an accusation against Moses, who prays and receives instructions that resolve the issue, at least temporarily. Here the names of the stops along the wilderness route are said to reflect the "complaining" and "testing" of the people. The issue in the wilderness is that Israel continues to confuse God with Santa Claus; a deity who does not produce on demand must be an absent deity or a non-entity. This attempt to manipulate God, to treat the Lord as a manifestation of their own will, is a precursor to the idolatry of the golden calf.

The Lord is leading the people, though Moses gets the blame when the water runs dry (vv. 1-2). This is ironic, since their salvation came via the sea — yet in the wilderness, they think that God has no command of the water. "Why did you bring us out of Egypt, to kill us and our children and livestock with thirst?" (v. 3). At least slavery had its benefits! Moses' cry in response, "They are almost ready to stone me" (v. 4) is also ironic in light of the subsequent command to strike a stone. The action itself is somewhat ludicrous — how could simply striking a rock produce water? However, the point is not the magic of the rod but the faithfulness of God. God has promised to provide for this people; despite their lack of faith and ingratitude, God will give them all they need.

Exodus points to the future when it describes "the rock at Horeb" (v. 6). Israel has not yet reached the mountain of God, but it looms over the story. God's provision will prove to be part of a covenant established with Israel, which is itself God's provision of life. Just as water flowed from the rock, life for Israel will flow from God's law. As we shall see in the gospel of John, the symbolism was not lost on subsequent generations of readers.

Romans 5:1-11

Romans 5 sits at the center of Paul's argument about how God is at work making human beings righteous through faith. The chapter is connected by theme and vocabulary to the four chapters that precede it, as it continues the discussion of what it means that "we are justified by faith" (v. 1). But it shares material as well as a basic format with the three following chapters: a basic statement concerning the meaning of justification, followed by further clarification of that statement. In chapter 5, Paul affirms that justification by faith produces a state of peace with God and reconciliation naturally follows from justification.

Paul uses all the rhetoric in his toolbox to make his point. Prominent in this section is the rhetorical "climax," a chain of phrases in which the last word of one phrase is picked up as the first word of the next. Paul's chain leads from suffering through endurance to character and hope (vv. 3-5); he thus affirms that "the sufferings of this present time are not worth comparing with the glory about to be revealed to us" (8:18). In verse 7 he uses the rhetorical device of "amplification" to demonstrate the extraordinary character of God's action in Christ, while in verses 9-11 he makes use of a lesser-to-greater argument to underline the implications of that action for our future.

Paul's argument so far has been that human beings are "justified" (or "made right") with God through the faithful action of Jesus, which we in turn share by faith (cf. 1:16-17; 3:21-26). This justification produces "peace with God," not a subjective feeling of peacefulness but an objective state of reconciliation, the cessation of hostilities between enemies (v. 1). Paul describes this state as "this grace" or "this gift" (*charis*, v. 2) in which we stand. It is "access" to a God who was literally our enemy (v. 10), because we were too weak to overcome our alienation from God (v. 6). We were in fact "sinners," those who had chosen not-God over God (cf. 1:18-32; 3:19-20, 23). Despite our alienated state, Christ died for us, resulting in justification, reconciliation, and salvation (vv. 6-10). This is our only basis for boasting, since none of this is dependent on our own actions, but everything on the initiation of God (vv. 2-3, 11).

Christ's faithful act has concrete results for those who share that faith. We have the "love of God... poured into our hearts" (v. 5). This does not refer to human affection for the deity, but to God's undiscriminating goodwill that becomes integrated into our lives through the power of the Holy Spirit (cf. ch. 8). God's love is transformative, in that it replicates specific characteristics in those who receive it: hope in the future, endurance through suffering, and a tested character (vv. 2-3). Paul's concern is for the future as well as the past, as he links reconciliation with "salvation," in the same way that Christ's death is linked to his resurrection (v. 10). Thus he sets up his argument in chapter 6 that participation in the death of Christ is also participation in his resurrection, meaning that Christians have died to sin and thus are able to live transformed lives.

John 4:5-42

John's narrative begs to be experienced rather than summarized, and nowhere is this more evident than in the story of the woman at the well in chapter 4. The story twists and turns as Jesus and the woman banter back and forth, and the "point" is to ride along with them, not to jump to a premature conclusion. The story reveals Jesus' identity as it goes along.

John's story has left the heart of the religious and social world of first-century Palestinian Judaism to head for its boondocks. Chapter 3 saw Jesus in Jerusalem, with John the Baptist testifying to his importance. Chapter 4, however, puts Jesus on the road to Galilee. Strikingly, he goes through rather than around Samaria — unheard of for the pious Jew, since Samaria was filled with foreigners and syncretists sent to colonize the area by Sargon of Assyria (cf. 2 Kings 17:24-34). The Samaritans had opposed the Jewish restoration of Jerusalem and had assisted in the persecutions of the Jews by the Syrians. At best, Samaritans were considered to be religious renegades. Yet Jesus' path takes him straight through this questionable region.

Even more questionable is Jesus' congress with a woman at Jacob's well. Not only do Jews "not share things in common with Samaritans" (v. 9), but men in general and rabbis in particular did not speak to strange women. In merely asking for water, Jesus has violated a number of social conventions! The woman is taken aback, but this momentary disorientation allows Jesus to focus the woman's attention on who he is (v. 10). The promise of "living water" not only reflects an ongoing biblical theme, highlighted in John (cf. Jeremiah 2:13, 17:13; Zechariah 14:8; John 7:37; Revelation 21:6), but is a pun of sorts, for "living water" was a common expression for running water, as opposed to a stagnant cistern. This sets the stage for a typical Johannine misunderstanding: the woman will think that Jesus is offering plumbing, where Jesus has something more symbolic in mind (vv. 11-12). Her question, "Are you greater than our ancestor Jacob?" (v. 12) shows that she does not understand the first thing about who Jesus is. But note that we the readers aren't much further ahead of her — we know that Jesus is in fact greater than Jacob, but we are not exactly clear what the symbolism of the water refers to (grace? revelation? the Spirit?). Jesus never fills in the blank for us — the imagery is left for us to ponder over, never flattened into a pat answer.

Jesus certainly puts Jacob in his place when he notes that "everyone who drinks of this water will be thirsty again" (v. 13). But that is not the case with the water Jesus carries: "The water that I will give will become in them a spring of water gushing up to eternal life" (v. 14). He has sold the goods — the woman definitely wants some of this stuff (after all, who wants to lug water jars back and forth?). The problem is that she has not fully understood what Jesus is offering — she asks for what she cannot fully comprehend, because she is still thinking in literal terms. Where Jesus is offering a life of grace, she sees only the freedom from household drudgery.

Jesus' reference to her husband is not a change of subject but a change of tactics. The woman still has not addressed the fundamental question of Jesus' identity. The question about her personal life will allow her to see correctly that he is a prophet (v. 19). The mention of five husbands — excessive even in that day — is not an attempt to highlight the woman's past life (sinful or not), but simply reinforces Jesus' stunning ability to see inside the heart. The woman's response is to engage Jesus on the level he has presented himself, as a prophet. Far from changing the subject, her question about the proper place of worship (v. 20) moves her back toward the crucial issue of Jesus' identity (in vv. 25-26). While John notes the superiority of the Jewish religion over that of the Samaritans (v. 22), the idea of worship has been transformed by God's new work in Jesus. The issue is now not a place, but "spirit and truth," both of which are to be found in Jesus (vv. 23-24).

The woman correctly perceives that this is a subject for the Messiah. The Samaritans expected the Messiah to be a teacher, so it is natural for the woman to affirm that "when he comes, he will proclaim all things to us" (v. 25). Her mention of the Messiah allows Jesus to bring the discussion full circle, as he reveals, "I am he (*ego eimi*), the one who is speaking to you" (v. 26). The woman did not need any more convincing — her previous conceptions of religion had been overturned: "Then the woman left her water jar and went back to the city" (v. 28).

Her report to the townsfolk, however, contains both a seed of exaggeration and a seed of doubt: "Come and see a man who told me everything I have ever done! He cannot be the Messiah, can he?" (v. 29). Her enthusiasm causes hyperbole, while her doubt is ever so subtly expressed in her question. Her faith is tentative, and yet sufficient for her to witness to others. As often in John, the focus shifts away once the witness has done her job: "Many Samaritans from that city believed in him because of the woman's testimony" (v. 39). Once again Jesus "stays" or "remains" (*meno*) with potential disciples, just as God "stays" with him (v. 40, cf. John 1:38-39; 2:12; 11:54; 14:10, 17, 25; 15:4-7, 9-10, 16; 21:22-23). This results in multiple conversions (v. 41), which the new believers attribute not to the woman's testimony, but to their own experience of Jesus (v. 42).

The woman's story illustrates the lesson that Jesus gives the disciples after her departure. She has become the (unlikely) sower who makes possible the later work of the reapers (vv. 35-38). Unfortunately, the disciples have the same problem of misunderstanding as the woman. They do not understand why he has broken social convention to speak to this woman (v. 27). Nor do they understand what he means when he says, "I have food to eat that you do not know about" (v. 32, note how the symbolic weight has shifted from water to its related necessity, food — the reverse of the movement in the Exodus story). Their lack of understanding is highlighted in their response, "Surely no one has brought him something to eat?" (v. 33). Jesus speaks in a more direct fashion to the disciples than he did to the woman, eliminating any misunderstanding at once: "My food is to do the will of him who sent me and to complete his work" (v. 34).

Application

I have always been intrigued by the woman's water jug. She came to the well to draw water but became so involved in her conversation with Jesus that she left the jug behind and ran away to tell everyone. She never does come back for it — it just sits there, all during Jesus' lecture to the disciples (and for all we know, during the whole two days he stayed in Samaria).

The jug, of course, plays a literary function by uniting the successive scenes in the story, even as the imagery shifts from drinking water to food. But the jug also serves a symbolic purpose. After all, Jesus did promise the woman "living water" that would lead to "eternal life." And she did leave her jug with him. I imagine him keeping his promise and filling the jug to the brim (cf. John 2:7).

As we have seen, even as the woman runs away, she hasn't quite made up her mind. The jug stands for the unfinished business between Jesus and the woman. The woman's jar remains by the well, because the story isn't through with her yet. It will never be through with her. She will keep coming back to Jesus for the living water that leads to eternal life, because it is not a one-shot inoculation. It involves "remaining" with Jesus. She has to leave her jar with him. He isn't done with her yet.

As the woman's story is open-ended, so is ours as readers. We must now decide how to respond to Jesus' self-revelation. And if we want the water he offers, we must leave our jars by the well for Jesus to refill. He's not done with us yet either.

An Alternative Application
Exodus 17:1-7; Romans 5:1-11; John 4:5-42. "Is the Lord among us or not?" The question posed by the

people of Israel did not have an obvious answer. The Israelites considered the lack of water to be a sign that God was not with them. Moses, on the contrary, considered their doubt a test of the Lord, which the Lord had no need to pass. God was with them, whether they realized it or not. The water was merely the sign that God had been there all along.

Paul echoes the sentiment when he includes suffering in a chain that leads to hope. For Paul, suffering is actually a matter for boasting, because it is a sign that God is indeed present. Why does Paul come to the exact opposite conclusion that the people of Israel did? Paul was influenced by Hellenistic philosophical traditions that saw suffering as educational; it produced endurance, which produced character, which produced hope. Far from bringing him to doubt, he took his suffering as proof of God's favor.

Jesus, too, understood that adverse outward conditions play no part in the assessment of one's spiritual health. He never did get that drink of water. Nor did he show any interest in the food his disciples brought from town. His sustenance was solely based on his obedient faith to God.

Believing is seeing

Sometimes we see people who are wide-eyed with wonder. Children especially can appear this way, in part because of the size of their eyeballs. Our eyeballs grow very little during the course of our lives and certainly not at the same rate as the rest of our bodies' organs. For that reason children stare at life with eyes bigger in proportion to their faces than those of adults. Compared with big people, children's eyes dominate their facial features and can thus appear more piercing and inquisitive.

While all five of our senses help us connect with our environment, we tend to rely more dependently on our sight than on smell, taste, hearing, or touch. We are people who trust our eyes before we will accept input from our other senses. Missouri claims that it is the "Show me!" state, and most of us take up residence there intellectually, whether we ever physically resettle into those borders. In fact, one of our favorite proverbs is "Seeing is believing!" Like Thomas among Jesus' disciples, we won't believe until the proof of something stares us in the face.

But sometimes sight blinds us. Rather than helping us understand life, our vision can distract us from reality. We find that in each of our passages for today. Samuel assesses each of the sons of Jesse in one way but does not find the next king of Israel until he begins to see with the unique eyes of God and believes in God's promises. The apostle Paul reminds us that physical sight and spiritual insight are not exactly the same thing and on the day that Jesus brought healing to a man who had been born blind, there was a great confusion about how people were to "see" this event.

While in much of our lives "seeing is believing," there are truly times when "believing is seeing." Today, you, as a pastor, must be in part a spiritual ophthalmologist who gives to your congregation an eye exam that improves the sight of every heart.

1 Samuel 16:1-13

Samuel's Israel is in chaos and the conflict has emerged from within the royal house itself. After Saul began his reign with great promise (1 Samuel 9-11), a number of events led both Samuel and Israel to question Saul's ability to rule well. First, Saul deliberately attacked a Philistine outpost to provoke war with Israel's much more powerful neighbor (1 Samuel 13:1-5). Then when Samuel was delayed in coming to the troops to confirm God's blessing on their fight, Saul jeopardized the religious pep rally by assuming a spiritual leadership for which he was not called or qualified (1 Samuel 13:8-13).

Next, Saul left the battlefield as if he were uncertain about the wisdom of the commotion he had set in motion (1 Samuel 13:14-15). When Saul's son Jonathan carried out a bold maneuver to resolve the tense standoff, Saul is caught indecisive and unprepared (1 Samuel 14:1-23). Furthermore, Saul shames himself before his troops, first by stupidly denying them any nourishment to carry on with the demands of battle (1 Samuel 14:24), and then later condemning his own son Jonathan to death when Jonathan disobeys this restriction that he had never heard in the first place (1 Samuel 14:25-44). Fortunately, Saul's armies had more sense than Saul and stopped this senseless abuse of power. But the tide had turned and both the nation and God fell out of alliance with Saul (1 Samuel 15).

Several people make judgments about David and his suitability for royal office in this short passage.

First, Samuel meets Jesse's oldest and strongest sons and assumes that they are the stuff of kings. God needs to remind Samuel that royalty is not determined merely by size and bearing. After all, Saul was handsome and stood head and shoulders above the rest of his community when Samuel had anointed him as king (1 Samuel 9:2). Samuel found out the fickleness of mere physical assessment, as Saul had become a burden to both him and Israel. Yet here Samuel was, again playing the beauty pageant game rather than waiting for the whisper that would help him to truly see the qualities of leadership that may be hidden inside the ugly or the unlikely. Only when he believes in the inner anointing of God on the true candidate will he be able to see David as king.

Then Jesse and the rest of his family also make a judgment about David. Evidently they think that David is a rascally runt who lacks the physique and maturity of his older brothers. Verse 11 is actually rather comical, if its implications are drawn out: first, the family doesn't think enough of David to allow him to be part of the great party that has come to town with Samuel's arrival. Next, they refuse to believe that Samuel's direct command to Jesse to assemble all his sons includes David (Can you imagine what an inferiority complex David could have gotten from being treated in such a way by his own parents?). Then when they finally remember that David is also part of the family, Jesse dismisses him offhandedly as merely "tending the sheep," as if his place is more with the hired servants than with the family. Jesse and his family believe David is not the stuff of leadership quality, and they sideline him from the selection process without a second thought. They do not believe in what David is truly made of, and therefore they cannot see him as king.

Thankfully, however, there is actually another onlooker. He does not make a cameo appearance in the story, but Samuel alludes to his presence. This other observer is God. While Samuel is uncertain as to what assessment God gives to each of the older sons of Jesse, he eventually becomes certain about God's measuring tools in the process and confident about God's ultimate choice: "The Lord does not look at the things man looks at. Man looks at the outward appearance, but the Lord looks at the heart" (v. 7). God understands the heart and qualities of David's life, and therefore God authorizes David's right to rule Israel. God believes in David and sees a king.

During this season of Lent, several themes from this passage may serve as helpful hooks on which to carry the sentiment of suffering. First, there is a deep-seated evil in our world that cannot be simply explained or excised. Saul's loss of his throne, the distresses in his family, his varied popular opinion polls, and his future are all complexly shifting around a variety of evils resident in the system. Saul's story at least requires us to think about the wiles of sin that confound all our daily lives. During Lent, we must take sin and evil seriously, and not minimize their contortions of God's good world.

Second, as David put it in Psalm 23, all of us will walk at one time or another through the "valley of the shadow of death" and be forced to eat at a table "in the presence of [our] enemies." This story in David's life echoes the misunderstandings and sufferings that we all share on the pilgrimage of life. Furthermore, it reminds us that the hardest thing we can do is walk the journey alone. Thus, to know that others have walked this way, including David and Jesus, we find some camaraderie, even in difficult times.

Third, there is the hopeful promise in Samuel's awareness of God's presence and constant direction. We may be surrounded by those who view us with scandalized eyes and torment us with inappropriate judgments, but one sees and knows and feels and has a heart disposed toward "good." It is precisely during Lent that we need to know that God believes in us as God's children, and therefore sees us with eyes of grace, mercy, and care.

Ephesians 5:8-14

Paul's letter to the Ephesians appears to have been a circular message of encouragement sent along with Tychicus (6:21-22) and the slave Onesimus (Colossians 4:7-9) whom Paul is returning to his master Philemon (Philemon 8-12). It was written while Paul was imprisoned (see 4:1), probably in Rome in the early '60s, and was likely meant to be circulated among the Christian congregations of the Lycus River Valley near Philemon's home (note that earliest manuscripts do not identify the recipients in 1:1, indicating that it may have gone to several churches before ending up in Ephesus; also see Colossians 4:16).

The letter is usually divided into two major parts, with chapters 1-3 explaining the supremacy of Christ in all things, and chapters 4-6 giving implications of Christ's rule for Christian living. In these verses, Paul deals with perceptions that change actions. There is no physical movement of Christ-believers from an arena lost in darkness (v. 8) into a realm constantly flooded with light. Instead, Paul wishes for his readers to understand the transformation of their mindsets and outlooks from one corrupted by sin into an intellectual and volitional perspective that is ruled again by God's original designs. Darkness is a spiritual condition that all of us are born into; light is the gift of God's grace in Jesus Christ and allows us to be reborn into a new moral and ethical posture toward ourselves and those around us.

Once we *believe*, we begin to *see* in new ways. Believing is seeing. During the season of Lent this takes tangible shape in the islands of grace that Sundays form in the dark morass of Lenten pain and suffering. The Sundays during Lent do not belong to the season of Lent, but are, in fact, early echoes of Easter victory. So on this fourth Sunday during Lent, it is important to remind our people that they may be surrounded by darkness, but they live as children of the light. The darkness presses in and causes turmoil, but the light of Christ is the guiding norm of our existence. We must, as one author has put it, "set our sights by the true North Star, Jesus."

John 9:1-41

While the synoptic gospels tell of many miracles that Jesus did, John enumerates only seven. He calls these "miraculous signs" (2:11) and tracks them moving the disciples and others from doubt to faith in Jesus as the Christ, as the Son of God, and as the Savior (John 20:30-31). Some Johannine scholars see a correlation between the seven signs and a rehearsal of Old Testament events. If that is so, the healing recorded in this passage is miraculous sign number six, and parallels the blindness of ancient Israel that could only be undone with God's interruptive coming on the "Day of the Lord" (see Isaiah 6:8-13; 9:2; 60:1-3; 61:1).

It is obvious from the start of this story that something unusual is happening, even for Jesus. While most miracles are done with a word or a touch, here Jesus goes through a strange process of several steps in order to bring sight to the blind man. First, he interprets the man's blindness not in causal terms as the disciples wanted to read it (9:1), but as a divinely ordained preparation for Jesus' own revelation (9:2). Second, Jesus places this healing in the context of the cosmological wrestling of darkness and light that are used to describe his coming in the prologue (1:1-18). Third, Jesus makes a mud pie of his spit and the clay of the earth in an act that seems reminiscent of the divine creative activity in Genesis 2:7, even to the point of dependency on divinely appointed moisture giving life to all things (Genesis 2:6). Fourth, the man's eyes are not opened immediately, but only after he goes to the pool of Siloam and washes off the mud packs. Of course, the only way he could get to the pool is by having family or friends guide him there, since he is still blind. This means that the act of healing would involve the presence, witness, and shared faith of others, placing the man into a believing community in order to receive his sight.

But the healing is met with confusion rather than faith. Many who had known the man in his blinded condition could not believe that the sighted man was the same person (9:8-9). Already this gives an indication as to how "believing" will be "seeing" for all in this story and not the other way around. Furthermore, it seems that John is giving a second message through the disbelief of the neighbors, namely that all who believe in Jesus as Savior have a new disposition about them that former acquaintances find confusing.

The incident becomes a matter for public debate. At stake is not the man's sight, but the character of Jesus. Is he a breaker of the Sabbath (9:14, 16)? Is he a common sinner like everyone else (9:16)? Is he a prophet (9:17)? Is he the Christ (9:22)? While the sign itself is undisputed, the message of the sign is debated. Jesus stands as a signpost, but all who gather around him argue as to what his signboard is declaring. Those who recognize his power believe in him as divinely sent (9:31-38); those who refuse to acknowledge their need for him deny Jesus' divine character and the healing he brings. In the end, the choice between blindness and sightedness is not physical but spiritual (9:39-41). Believing is seeing.

In order to tie this to our journey through Lent it might be appropriate to make a connection with those things in our lives that confuse, confound, and torment us: a threatening disease, a sudden death, a broken marriage, a moral failure of someone we trusted, a lack of work, a terrifying terrorist attack. Why these? Why me? Why us? Why now? Just as with the man's blindness in John's story, we can get caught up in micro-assessments and lose sight of the big picture. Jesus came to share our walk with us, as marked by our Lenten remembrances, but he came as a sign of the big picture of healing that God was providing for our darkened world. Each incident of evil is of concern to God, but no single happenstance of cruelty or disease ought to detract us from the important goal of God — the total restoration of God's creation. During Lent we can get caught up in our shared sufferings with Jesus. What we need to remember is their redemptive purpose.

A second theme from this story is that of the community of faith. While the formerly blind man has great trust in Jesus, his original healing came only through a communal effort to get him to the waters of Siloam. Furthermore, there is a communal ownership of the outcomes of faith — the man's parents fear being expelled from the synagogue as a result of their connection with their son. To John's first readers this message likely resonated in their current situation and called them to communities of faithfulness over against the communities of persecution that threatened them. We in North America tend to view faith and belief as personal, individual matters. The truth is that we cannot walk either through Lenten suffering or Easter hope alone. We need community.

Application

Believing is seeing. It was so for the characters that surrounded the boy David when even his family did not recognize his true worth. It was true for Paul's readers who attempted to live according to divine ethics in a world contorted by devilish designs. It was also this way for the many people who saw the miraculous sign of Jesus in John 9, and who chose to respond with different faith perspectives.

So, too, it is with us. Every year we take this torturous pilgrimage through Lent, bent with the burdens of sin and evil clinging to us. Sometimes it feels good to wallow in misery. There is a psychological desire in each of us to want to play the martyr, to cry for others to pity us, and to lament the uniqueness of our particular load of injustice and hurt. These passages remind us that what we see is not necessarily what we get, and what we experience will not be the last chapter written about our condition. When we believe, we see things anew. When we understand God's perspectives and designs, we move from slugging it out in the shadows to life in the light, and the turning point is not merely some pious wish or some psychological self-babble or some political promising, but rather the person of Jesus. Who is Jesus? Is Jesus the Son of God, the divine messenger, the physician of the soul? Or is Jesus merely another "sinner" among us who taunts us with false pledges? Those who trust Jesus may not be able to explain it, but neither do they stumble in darkness any longer.

Lent 5
Ezekiel 37:1-14
Romans 8:6-11
John 11:1-45
by David Kalas

No spring chicken

Each year about this time, we in the church are fond of making a misplaced analogy. Tennyson wrote, "In the spring a young man's fancy lightly turns to thoughts of love." Perhaps if he had observed the contemporary American church, he would have written, "In the spring a preacher's fancy turns to thoughts of nature and Easter." Again and again each March or April, we see trotted out the symbolic connection between the event we celebrate on Easter — Christ's resurrection — and the season in which we celebrate it — springtime. Spring, we are told, is the season of new life, and so the resurrection of Christ is tied to nature's annual display of spring flowers and buds on trees.

The association between Easter and spring is a lovely one and quite sentimental. Unfortunately, it is also quite misleading. Christ's resurrection is not at all paralleled by nature. Christ's resurrection was, in fact, entirely unnatural and to make the association between the two is to apply the wrong analogy, and therefore to perpetuate a misunderstanding.

Our three lections for this week invite us to ponder the issue of dead things being brought back to life. Ezekiel witnesses a startling demonstration of that event in the valley of dry bones. Jesus brings dead Lazarus back to life, and Paul bears witness to the Spirit "who raised Christ from the dead" and who will do the same for us. We have the opportunity this week to set aside the beauty of what nature does each spring and see, in contrast, the beauty of what God does, what Christ did, and what the Spirit will do in us.

Ezekiel 37:1-14

A marvelous matrix of relationships is contained here in this familiar passage, and any of the relationships could be explored by the preacher to great effect.

There is, first, the relationship between Ezekiel and God. We could be endlessly fascinated by the biblical accounts of how God deals with his servants, for it gives us fresh insight into our own relationship with him. In this instance, we have the fascinating appellation consistently used by God for Ezekiel, *ben adam*. The NRSV translates the Hebrew phrase as "mortal," while the KJV, RSV, NIV, and NKJV all opt for "son of man." The Septuagint's translation (*huie anthropou*) seems to favor a "son of man" or "son of mankind" reading. Meanwhile, the Living Bible's paraphrase is perhaps more picturesque: "son of dust." Whatever the best translation, the title offers deliberate perspective and constant reminders to Ezekiel of who and what he is. It is not belittling; it is merely a reminder of fact, and a reminder that we and our native egocentricity need God.

The irresistibly appealing hallmark of Ezekiel's relationship with God, meanwhile, is its personal and dialogical quality. Most of the book is written in the first-person, which gives the account a very personal flavor. The personal testimony offered there is of a God who almost continuously speaks with Ezekiel. Nearly thirty times, the prophet recalls that the Lord "said to me," and it is not a one-way lecture, but more of a guided tour. Again and again throughout the book, as in our selected passage, the Lord shows Ezekiel things (e.g., 44:5), invites him to go and see (e.g., 8:5; 8:9), or asks him if he has seen (e.g., 8:17).

Even if the *ben adam* term is "off-putting" to us at first, the actual playing out of the relationship that we see between God and Ezekiel has a terrifically personal quality to it. The Lord is walking the prophet through a series of lessons, like a tutor, and it is experiential and conversational, at that. Our particular passage certainly has that quality. God does not merely say to Ezekiel what he wants Ezekiel to know — or, a step further removed, what he wants his people to know. Rather, Ezekiel and the Lord experience the event together.

Next, we have the relationship between Ezekiel and the bones. That is an impersonal relationship, to be sure, but it is one that may resonate with our experience. We, and the people in our pews, will from time to time, look out over a hopeless landscape, and what shall be our relationship to that inanimate despair? Will we wave the white flag at what is an obviously lost cause? Will we shrug our shoulders in dismay? Or will we open our minds to the possibilities of what God can do, following his instructions all the way to new life in the midst of dried up and dismembered death?

Then there is the relationship between Ezekiel and the people of Israel. It turns out that they are the ones represented by that hopeless valley of dry and detached bones. The experience in the valley was meant by God to be a kind of training exercise for Ezekiel. Like the astronaut who goes through all sorts of simulation experiences on earth before being launched into outer space, so God walked Ezekiel through a simulation of what his ministry must be: prophesying in the midst of hopelessness and despair; believing upstream; and participating in the miraculous work, word, and will of God.

Finally there is the relationship between God and his people Israel. That is the central issue, of course. The entire ministry and message of the prophet are subsets of this larger matter: God's relationship to his people. That relationship is, we discover, an uneven two-way street. Love and loyalty flow in both directions, but the volume is so very much greater going one way than the other.

God's people had been scandalously disloyal to him, and their unfaithfulness is chronicled and condemned in earlier chapters of Ezekiel. So, too, are the details of God's judgment on his people for their infidelity. In the end, however, the Lord does not abandon his people. They deserve to be divorced, to be sure, but that is not God's choice. They deserve to be utterly crushed, but instead he preserves a remnant. So here, in this episode, the people are represented by the brokenness and hopelessness of the valley of dry bones, but God will not leave his people in that condition. Rather, as only he can do, we read that the Lord will "open your graves, and bring you up from your graves... and you shall live."

Romans 8:6-11

The operative word in verses 6 and 7 is not immediately apparent in most translations. The King James and New King James Versions render the first part of verse 6: "For to be carnally minded is death." Meanwhile, the Revised Standard and New Revised Standard Versions take a slightly different approach: "To set the mind on the flesh is death." The New English Bible, by contrast, reads: "Those who live on the level of our lower nature have their outlook formed by it, and that spells death."

If a person in your congregation sat down and read several such English translations side-by-side, he or she might be confused. The various translations lead one to think that there must be a very complex verb in the original Greek. It seems to be a verb that can be variously translated as "to be," "to set the mind," or "to live on the level of."

In fact, however, what lies behind the different translations is not a very complex Greek verb, but rather no Greek verb at all.

The New International Version, in this case, may come nearest to giving the sense of it: "The mind of sinful man is death." Even the English word "is" represents an insertion, for the Greek has no verb at all. Rather, the construction of verse 6 simply juxtaposes two subjects and in the absence of a verb it almost suggests the mathematical sign for "equals" in between.

Read literally, verse 6 would run like this: "For the mind of the flesh death, and the mind of the Spirit life and peace."

The original Greek word that Paul uses, which I have translated above as "mind," is not the standard New Testament Greek word for "mind." Rather, it is a word that appears only three times in the entire New Testament, and all three occurrences are right here in Romans 8 (vv. 6, 7, and 27). It is perhaps more satisfactory to translate it as "mindset" or "way of thinking."

It is really just two equations that Paul presents: The way of thinking of the flesh equals death; the way of thinking of the Spirit equals life and peace. "You do the math," Paul says in effect. If our mindset is of the flesh, it follows naturally that we will not submit to God's law and cannot please God, so we are invited to have the mindset of the Spirit.

The other fascinating intersection of grammar and theology in this passage is found in the use of the preposition "in." On the one hand, Paul says that the Christians to whom he is writing are not "in the flesh" but rather "in the Spirit." On the other hand, he also notes that "the Spirit of God dwells in you." Moreover, "if the Spirit... dwells in you," becomes the key to the resurrection of the body.

There are no special things to be said about the Greek preposition involved here. It is not uncommon or profound. Our English "in" is an adequate translation of it, but its recurring usage here does invite the preacher to ponder these three realities: our being in the flesh, our being in the Spirit, and the Spirit being in us.

The reference to the resurrection within this context suggests another kind of mathematical equation. The church has, for years, struggled with the relationship of our works and our salvation. Even apart from the in-depth theological debates throughout church history, there are the over-the-back-fence theologians who also weigh in on the subject. They, the folks in our culture who believe that there is a heaven, find it almost irresistible to assume that it's "good people" who go there.

The components of this passage, however, suggest another factor that can help the equation to make sense. That factor is the Spirit. Rather than limping along with the happy but somewhat shallow assumption that folks who live good lives will go to heaven, we see in Paul's understanding that the Spirit is actually the key. Namely, it is the Spirit that engenders righteous living, and it is the Spirit that raises us from the dead. We might conclude, therefore, that our salvation is not the by-product of our good lives, but rather our good lives and our salvation are both products of the Spirit's work within us.

John 11:1-45

The preaching potential of John 11 is staggering. I'm a believer that the whole Bible is worth preaching — every book, every chapter — but I will quickly concede that the sermon material is a bit more obvious in some passages than in others. In John 11, there are more sermons than one Sunday can accommodate. So many larger themes come into play in this passage.

First, there is the relationship between Jesus and this particular family — Mary, Martha, and Lazarus. In addition to this episode, we have at least two other glimpses into this group of friends (Luke 10:38-42; John 12:1-11).

Second, we are met, again, here with this matter of purpose. Jesus does not merely chalk up Lazarus' sickness and death to the natural order but rather claims that "it is for God's glory, so that the Son of God may be glorified through it." The teaching is reminiscent of the healing of the blind man earlier in John's gospel, when Jesus explains, "He was born blind so that God's works might be revealed in him" (John 9:3).

Third, this occasion is part of the larger plot of Jesus' opponents who seek to kill him. The disciples were conscious of this issue (John 11:8), though it is interesting that danger, fear, and opposition, which can be primary factors in most human decision-making, do not play a part in where Jesus goes or what Jesus does. Also, just beyond the boundaries of our selected passage, Lazarus' return to life becomes another point of controversy and consternation for Jesus' opponents.

Fourth, there is the faith-crisis issue of God's timing. This is not limited to some theoretical theme in scripture, of course; this is a daily faith issue for the people in our pews. Early in the episode, we see Jesus deliberately delaying his trip to Bethany. Later, observers at Lazarus' tomb asked, "Could not he who opened the eyes of the blind man have kept this man from dying?" (v. 37). And, in the most poignant, human moment of all, both Martha and Mary individually lament to Jesus, "Lord, if you had been here, my brother would not have died" (vv. 21, 32).

Finally, this passage features one of the "I am" statements of Jesus. These statements are a significant theme in John's gospel, accumulating and cooperating to reveal who Jesus is, which is the real issue of the gospel. What Jesus said and did are reported, it seems, as a means to that larger end: recognizing who Jesus is and the occasion of Lazarus' death yields one of the most famous of those statements: "I am the resurrection and the life" (v. 25).

Application

We have often used the surrounding context of springtime as a metaphor for the resurrection we celebrate at Easter. As we consider the three death-to-life passages we have before us today, we should consider a revamping of the analogy. Use nature's springtime not in comparison with but in contrast to Christ's resurrection.

At springtime, we say, nature shows signs of new life. The flowers begin to poke through the ground and the branches on the trees show the buds of new leaves. That's all very lovely, of course, but it is not resurrection. It is not even resuscitation.

Ezekiel was confronted with what must have been a horrid sight: a valley full of dry bones. Every syllable of the phrase connotes death, doesn't it? We already figuratively associate death with a valley. The bones are surely a symbol of death, and the fact that they are just scattered bones — not assembled skeletons — makes them seem still further removed from life. Finally, they are dry. Whenever they were alive, it was a long time ago.

Lazarus had not been dead so long, of course, but it was long enough. Long enough that he had been wrapped up and buried. Long enough that the tomb was sealed off with a stone. Long enough that the ever-fastidious Martha was concerned about the stench.

How shall we set nature side-by-side with Ezekiel's valley? How shall we take springtime and contrast it with Lazarus?

Ezekiel's valley would not be full of trees that are bare in the winter — for those trees are still alive. No, Ezekiel's valley would be full of leaves that have turned brown, fallen off, and been mulched. For those leaves to come together, turn green, and reattach themselves to trees — that would not be nature and springtime but would be Ezekiel's dry bones coming to life again.

Lazarus' tomb would not have an empty garden within it waiting for spring to bring dormant bulbs to bloom. No, Lazarus' tomb would have within it the bagged clippings from last month's lawn mowing. It would be dead, yellowed, stale, and smelly. Jesus calls in and the bag bounces out. "Tear it open," he commands, and we find the clippings alive, verdant, and growing.

What God did at the valley of dry bones was not natural. What Jesus did at Lazarus' tomb was not natural. What the Spirit did at the empty tomb was not natural. It is not mimicked by spring.

What Christ can do in our lives — and in our deaths — is not bound by the limitations of nature or dictated by the natural order. Because real resurrection and life are not found in nature: they are found in him.

An Alternative Application

Ezekiel 37:1-14. Typically a question raises doubts. A question challenges our certainty. Are you sure? Can you prove it? But what if...?

We see the phenomenon at work right from the beginning. The serpent asked a question in an effort to raise doubts in Eve's mind. "Did God say, 'You shall not eat from any tree in the garden'?" (Genesis 3:1). Well, no. No, that's not at all what God said. But the question raised that bit of doubt in Eve's mind: a doubt about God, on which the serpent later expanded and capitalized.

The writer of Proverbs observes, "The first man to speak in court always seems right until his opponent begins to question him" (Proverbs 18:17 TEV). So it is that a question typically raises doubts.

When Ezekiel stands before his own Death Valley, however, God asks a question that points in a different direction. "Can these bones live?"

If the question came from anyone else, it would be an insult, an offense, salt in the wound. Walk into the lawyer's office where the divorce papers are being signed and ask, "Can this marriage be saved?" Stand in the hospital room beside what remains of a disease-riddled body, struggling through its final breaths, and ask, "Can this person be healed?" Preposterous questions.

But God's question is meant to raise a wholesome doubt in Ezekiel's mind. Or perhaps it was something else. Surely doubt already prevailed in the face of that panorama of death. Can you raise a doubt about doubt? God asked a question to raise faith in Ezekiel's mind!

As we noted above, both we and the people in our pews might — today, tomorrow, or one day soon — look out over a seemingly hopeless landscape. The hymn writer encourages us to "ponder anew what the almighty can do, if with his love he befriend thee" ("Praise to the Lord, the Almighty" by Joachim Neander, translated by Catherine Winkworth). We might help ourselves ponder anew what the Lord can do by asking questions — preposterous questions, outlandish questions, questions that raise faith.

Can this marriage be saved? Can this body be healed? Can this addiction be broken? Can this person ever change?

Can these bones live?

Passion / Palm Sunday (Lent 6)
Isaiah 50:4-9a
Philippians 2:5-11
Matthew 26:14—27:66
by William Shepherd

The wrong anthem

The choir director was aghast. "I just didn't realize," she said. "It was totally inappropriate. I chose the wrong anthem."

Her mistake was understandable. The service schedule said, "Palm Sunday," and the usual Palm Sunday choir anthem includes shouts of "Hosanna." The problem was the placement. In the *Book of Common Prayer*, the "Hosanna" part comes at the beginning of the service. Following a procession with singing and palm-waving, the congregation settles down to a much more grave matter: a participatory reading of one of the passion narratives from the synoptic gospels. The choir director's anthem, coming after this solemn reading, did seem a bit inappropriate.

Yet Palm Sunday and Passion Sunday are one and the same, and today's readings all describe the same Messiah, and the same God who is defined by that Messiah: One who is self-giving to a fault. The difference between the triumphal entry into Jerusalem and the crucifixion is simply that the definition of messiahship has been clarified; it is not to be manifested in the royal palace, but among the poor, the weak, and the neglected. Whatever historical reality may underlie these stories, on this day we read about a humble king who is humbled further, and we enact our own participation in these stories by taking the part of "the crowd" in both stories. The same crowd that shouts "Hosanna to the Son of David!" will soon shout, "Crucify him!"

Isaiah 50:4-9a

The Third Servant Song in Second Isaiah is a monologue, with the Servant as the speaker. The monologue reflects the broader genre of a trust psalm; the Servant expresses his trust in God. Here in Isaiah, the Servant should be thought of as the embodiment of Israel (or the faithful remnant in Israel) and not as an individual (cf. 48:16; 49:3).

The passage in which our lection occurs is divided into three sections. The introduction (vv. 1-3) shares with the previous chapter the invocation of Zion but now it is specifically the "children of Zion" who are called (v. 1). The speaker poses questions that will be answered in the Song proper (vv. 4-9). The final verses (vv. 10-11) are a commentary in response to the Song (here the Servant is no longer the speaker): The community is divided in their response to the Servant, and those who do not believe are warned of dire consequences.

The Servant is empowered by God "to sustain the weary with a word" (v. 4). Specifically, the Servant is given an ear for the gift of God's word: "The Lord God has given me the tongue of those who are taught" (the NRSV translation, "tongue of a teacher," is possible, but not likely). What the Servant is learning here is not information as much as lifestyle; the community is taught to accept suffering and shame on God's behalf (v. 5). "I gave my back to those who struck me, and my cheeks to those who pulled out the beard; I did not hide my face from insult and spitting" (v. 6). Despite this trial, the community asserts its faith: "The Lord God helps me; therefore I have not been disgraced; therefore I have set my face like flint, and I know that I shall not be put to shame" (v. 7). The Servant uses legal language to picture his exoneration, with God sitting in the defense attorney's chair: "He who vindicates me is near" (v. 8). The prosecution's witnesses are faulty ("Who are my adversaries?"), and the judge will find no guilt (v. 9).

With this vivid picture of personal suffering, Second Isaiah embodies both the grief and hope of a community that had suffered badly in exile. No wonder Christians understood this passage to reflect and interpret the life and death of their Messiah!

Philippians 2:5-11

The Song continues in Paul's letter to the Philippians. Most scholars see this passage as a literal song, an early Christian hymn inserted by Paul into his letter as support for his exhortation. This is certainly possible. The unusual and poetic vocabulary may not be Paul's own, and the structure is reminiscent of Hebrew poetry in its stress and parallelism (it is usually thought to be influenced by Isaiah's Servant Songs, though some scholars see its primary background in the story of Adam's fall in Genesis). However, the themes and even the language are well within Paul's rhetorical repertoire, so he may have written this ode to Christ himself.

Clearly the hymn moves in two directions: first downward in humility, then upward to glory. It is not so clear what this movement actually represents. Traditional interpretation has seen here a reference to the pre-existence and incarnation of Christ, who came down from heaven to take human form, and then returned from whence he came. But an equally good case could be made that the poetic language imagines no pre-existence, and that the entire tale is told of the incarnate Christ, who humbled himself in service to others. Both interpretations fit the hymn (though I incline to the traditional one).

Neither is there a consensus on how the main focus of the hymn is to be understood. The crux here is the elliptical opening sentence, which reads literally "This think in you (pl.) which also in Christ Jesus" (v. 5). The verb must be supplied in the second half of the sentence. Traditionally, the simplest translation has been preferred, with the verb "to be" (so NRSV, "Let the same mind be in you that was in Christ Jesus"). This implies that the point is simply ethical imitation, and the life of the community should parallel the life of Christ ("in you" is best understood as "among yourselves," specifying not individual inner disposition but group character). However, this translation does not quite capture all the nuances of Paul's expression "in Christ," which indicates a state of union and power that goes beyond mere aping of actions. We might translate the phrase, "which is yours as those who are in Christ," or "which you think as those who are in Christ" (supplying the verb from the first half of the sentence). The sentence could be taken in a number of ways, as paradigmatic (Christ providing the model mind), mystical (the mind shared in union with Christ), ecclesiastical (the mind of those who are the Body of Christ), or soteriological (the mind that comes from being "in Christ"). These different ways of understanding the introductory sentence are not necessarily contradictory, however — in fact, they are quite complementary. Following Jesus is not merely imitating his example but participating in his life and being energized by his power. It is not just that we follow Christ but that we are in some sense sharers in Christ's nature and power, which the hymn specifies.

However we understand the introduction, we must understand how the hymn functions as part of Paul's argument. Philippians is a letter about friendship and possessions and how one expresses the other. Paul writes to his friends to thank them for their monetary gift (1:7; 4:10, 15-18); it is not going too far to say that Philippians is one long thank-you note! In Greco-Roman society, it was a common notion that "friends share all things," and Paul rightly takes their gift as a sign of that kind of friendship. His exhortation to them is to live out the implications of their gift of friendship by sharing their hearts and minds. Paul then evokes several examples of the kind of mindset he is commending: Jesus (2:5-11), Timothy and Epaphroditus (2:19—3:1), and Paul himself (3:20—4:1). In this case, he starts his examples with the climax, pulling out all the rhetorical guns to exhort them to "make my joy complete: be of the same mind, having the same love, being in full accord and of one mind" (2:2).

The "one mind" they are to share is the mind of Christ, which is described in the hymn. He was, first of all, in "the form of God." Traditionally, this has been understood as a reference to the divine Christ's pre-existence, but it could refer to his human form, as Adam was created in "the image of God." In either case, he did not regard that form as *harpagmos*, "something to be seized, grasped, robbed," such as booty or plunder (v. 6). The poetic idea here is that Christ chose not to use his gifts to his own advantage; he did not take the opportunity that they presented for self-promotion. Note that this is "possessions" language, and that the "possessions" symbolize a spiritual state, a notion that probably would not be lost on a congregation that had so recently sacrificed their own goods for Paul's mission.

Rather than looking out for himself, Christ "emptied himself" or stripped himself of the privileges that came with his status (like a reverse Adam). He took on the identity of a slave, much like Isaiah's Servant (the hymn uses several synonyms for "form" and "likeness," all of which are poetic variants of the same idea). He did not thereby cease to be in the form of God but by doing so defined that form — it is that of a slave (v. 7). The slave is humble and obedient (here the stark contrast to Adam), and Paul takes the logic of his argument to its obvious conclusion: the ultimate emptying and humbling is found in a death on the cross (v. 8).

Having reached the bottom, the movement is reversed (v. 9). The humble Christ is exalted and given "the name that is above every name," either the name "Jesus" (v. 10) or more likely "Lord" (v. 11). This leads to a cosmic proclamation, in which "every knee should bend, in heaven and on earth and under the earth, and every tongue should confess that Jesus Christ is Lord, to the glory of God the Father" (vv. 10-11). The entire universe is thus brought under the lordship of Christ. On the basis of this declaration, Paul will launch further into his exhortation, which includes not only the request for good works but also the promise of God's assistance (vv. 12-13).

Matthew 26:14—27:66

The long passion narrative in Matthew is dependent on the tradition passed along by Mark (which in turn is similar to the Johannine framework; no doubt a common oral tradition stands behind both). It is set during the Jewish Passover, with its symbolism of the sacrificial lamb. The Passover was a pilgrimage feast, during which a great many visitors would come to Jerusalem; this sets the scene for the explosive political machinations that lead to the cross. Like many other Passover pilgrims, Jesus and his disciples have to find a place to eat the feast, but their feast will soon turn to sorrow. The synoptics picture Jesus being tried and executed on the night of the Passover meal (John's alternate chronology is considered by many to be more historically likely).

Matthew manages to add his own unique touches to the traditional framework. He makes a number of editorial changes to his source; for example, he makes the order of the mockery before the cross more logical (27:27-44). He tends to simplify Mark but is not averse to adding adjectives (27:57, 59-60) and even whole scenes (27:1-10, 62-66). He rearranges things in light of the current practice of his Jewish-Christian community; for example, in his account of the Last Supper, the words of institution reflect later liturgical practice and the actions have been condensed and merged into one ceremony of bread and cup in the middle of the meal. His major changes, however, have to do with broad theological concerns.

Foremost of these Matthean themes is the fulfillment of prophecy. In Matthew, Jesus is presented as a teacher of Torah, but also as himself the fulfillment of Torah. Jesus is himself a prophet whose words prove true again and again (26:17-18, 21-29, 31-35, 45-46). This is because God has planned and is in control of all these events. The episode of the severed ear illustrates God's control: When one of the disciples draws a sword and strikes the slave of the high priest, Jesus immediately orders the cessation of all violence in his defense. "Do you think that I cannot appeal to my Father, and he will at once send me more than twelve legions of angels? But how then would the scriptures be fulfilled, which say it must happen this way?" (26:53-54). Less important than what particular scriptures Matthew had in mind here (he probably refers to Zechariah 13:7) is simply *that* all these events are the fulfillment of scripture. God has planned it this way all along, and the scriptures show the way. Thus they are cited often (26:15, 24, 31, 54, 56; 27:9-10,

46) and even when they are not cited explicitly, they are alluded to (note especially the broad allusions to Psalms 22 and 69 in the crucifixion and death scenes).

That God is in control is part and parcel with Matthew's concern with eschatology, the coming of the last days. Though on a human level, it is Judas who has "handed over" (*paradidomi*, usually translated "betrayed") Jesus, actually it is God who is doing the handing (the same verb, *paradidomi*, is used in the "divine passive" in 26:2). God is handing over the Son on behalf of the whole world. This is happening in eschatological time, *kairos*, as Jesus himself admits when he says, "My time is near" (26:18). As foretold in the prophets, there will be a heavenly banquet in these last days (26:29). What Jesus is doing here, as Matthew sees it, is ushering in the end of the age. Other instances of eschatological imagery include the legion of angels (26:53), the portents attending the crucifixion and resurrection (27:51-53; cf. Ezekiel 37:1-4), and the appearance of Elijah to "save" Jesus (27:49).

Matthew is unique in his concentration on the role of Judas in God's plan. Only Matthew includes the tradition that pictures Judas' interaction with the Jewish leaders (27:1-10). In contrast with the woman who lavishes expensive ointment on Jesus (26:14), Judas "hands over" Jesus for a paltry sum. His "kiss" proves hollow, used only as an identifying mark in the Passover hubbub. His words show his true nature, as he identifies Jesus with a term used only by Jesus' enemies in Matthew, never by his disciples: "Rabbi" (26:25, 48-49). Jesus in response gives him a sarcastic "Friend" (probably the equivalent of "Bub") and asserts God's control over the whole process: "Do what you are here to do" (26:50).

Judas may be culpable, but Matthew leaves no doubt which human agency is ultimately responsible. Pilate is let off easily, although historically crucifixion was a punishment used only by the Romans. Matthew even brings in a scene with Pilate's wife to lessen his culpability (27:19). The scene of Pilate washing his hands (27:24) is almost laughable; no one got to that level of power in the Roman Empire with clean hands, and we know Pilate's ruthlessness from other contemporary sources. But Matthew, whose community was deeply in conflict with the synagogue, placed the blame squarely on Jewish shoulders, to the point of having the people as a whole cry, "His blood be upon us and on our children" (27:25).

All along, though, Jesus is presented as a sacrificial innocent. He is declared "innocent" again and again (cf. 26:58-59, 66; 27:18-19, 23-24). In Passover imagery, he speaks of his death as a sacrifice for sins (26:28). Throughout the process, he remains in total control (26:18-19, 21-29, 45; 27:14). He lives — and dies — only according to God's plan.

Application

People are surprised when I tell them that I don't believe in preaching on Palm Sunday. They think I'm kidding but I'm not. The passion narrative is long and intense. If read in parts and with congregational participation, it can be emotionally draining. The last thing I want to see at the end of it is some preacher belaboring the point (or worse yet, telling a joke).

Which is not to say that there should be no explication of the text on Palm Sunday. I propose replacing the sermon with a short introduction to the passion narrative that precedes rather than follows the reading. The introduction could point the congregation to what they should be listening for (particularly the unique emphases of Matthew's version). It would set them up to properly hear the reading. Following the reading there should be extended silence to let it soak in.

The usual objection to my "No Sermon Palm Sunday" is that "the people might need help applying the text to their lives." But that is really the point, isn't it? The congregation must work out their own salvation with fear and trembling (Philippians 2:12). The passion narrative provides the model for all of Christian life; it is not "applied" so much as it *is* that life. Jesus' death provides the model for the life of faith, as his resurrection assures the power to be faithful. The passion narrative is the gospel in a nutshell: He gave himself for us so that we could give ourselves for him.

An Alternative Application

Matthew 26:14—27:66. The great Jewish scholar Samuel Sandmel used to tell this story: A Jew is walking down the street on Palm Sunday. All of a sudden, a Christian comes out of church and starts beating the Jew on the head.

"Why are you hitting me?" the Jew asks. "What have I done to you?"

"You Jews killed Jesus," says the Christian.

"That was 2,000 years ago!" says the Jew.

"Well," says the Christian, "I just found out today."

Sandmel and others, both Jews and Christians, would conclude that reading the New Testament is a very dangerous thing, and as we know, the Bible is a dangerous book to read. But it's supposed to be dangerous to us, not to others.

One problem with preaching today is that the church doesn't do enough to challenge outlandish interpretations of the gospels. We should protest the notion that God blames the Jewish people for Jesus' death. Matthew wrote as part of a broader interreligious fight, in which the Gentile church was asserting itself in contrast to its Jewish roots. As with all such internecine conflicts, the rhetorical juices flowed. We should not take the depictions of the Pharisees, Sadducees, and Jewish people in the gospels as gospel truth. It is polemic, slanted, and a bit unfair.

At the very least, we should tell our congregations this: Do not, repeat, do not march out of church looking to beat up a Jew. Do not blame the Jews. Do not let prejudice, stupidity, and violence rule your hearts. Christ died for all of us, so that we might walk in new life.

Maundy Thursday
Exodus 12:1-4 (5-10) 11-14
1 Corinthians 11:23-26
John 13:1-17, 31b-35
by David Kalas

Long table

Perhaps you've been part of a large group going out to eat together. You arrive at the restaurant and they don't have a single table that can accommodate the whole group. The hostess asks you to wait for a moment, and she combines efforts with several of the servers to rearrange some of the vacant tables and chairs, pushing tables together to create one long table for your oversized party.

I recall several occasions when I have been part of such a group. I've even seen restaurants assign more than one server to our "table" because it was so populated.

Such occasions are usually very jovial — lots of conversation and laughter. If, by chance, you have a moment when you aren't part of a conversation, then you have the leisure to look down the long table and see the all the faces of these cherished friends and family members, gathered together in fellowship.

Of course, a very long table is somewhat impractical for conversation. You can't easily converse with someone who is clear at the other end. Still, there is something satisfying about sitting all together — a feeling of connectedness that is missing when your group is scattered over several different tables and booths.

Conjure up the images of such a long and loving table for your congregation this night, for that is where we sit. We gather this evening at a very long table, indeed — and getting longer every day. For this is a table that does not merely stretch across part of a room: it spans generations and centuries. We cannot even calculate the number of people seated there.

Yet our scripture passages for this holy day will help us to pause our conversation, to look up and down the table, and to see the faces of the cherished family and friends who are gathered for fellowship with our host.

Exodus 12:1-4 (5-10) 11-14

The far end of our very long table stretches back over 3,000 years. Our first task is to squint our eyes to try to see the folks all the way at that other end. There they are: Moses and the Hebrew slaves in Egypt.

People who pay some attention to the liturgical or church calendar will appreciate the Lord's instruction in verse 2. Speaking of the current month — that is, the month that the Israelites celebrated the Passover and left Egypt — the Lord said, "It shall be the first month of the year for you." One senses that, perhaps prior to this time, that particular month was not regarded as the first month on the Hebrew calendar. So the Israelites made an adjustment that is reminiscent of what we do in the church: namely, while the calendar says that the new year begins in January, and while the schools say that the new year begins in late August or early September, in the church we affirm that the new year begins with Advent. For the Hebrews, the new year began in the month of the Passover.

Next, God gave the people instructions for preparing and eating the Passover meal. We are accustomed to instructions for preparing food: We call them recipes. When it comes to eating the food, however, the only sort of instructions we get in most cases is the training in manners that our parents provided. "Elbows off the table." "Napkin in your lap." "Feet on the floor." "Chew with your mouth closed." And such.

Against such standard fare, God's instructions seem quite strange. For, if anything, the instructions from God seem to us rather unmannerly. We picture people wolfing down their food while wearing their overcoats and holding their car keys. It seems to us both an impolite and an unhealthy way to eat.

Over the millennia, the Jewish celebration of the Passover meal has become so rich with symbolic acts and liturgical elements that it is anything but "fast food." In that original context in Egypt, however, the key element was speed. "You shall eat it hurriedly," God told the people, for after centuries of waiting, now their deliverance was going to come quickly.

God's statement that "on all the gods of Egypt I will execute judgments" is a fascinating insight into the Passover event, if not the meal itself. At a purely human level, of course, we don't see the gods of Egypt in the picture at all. It is the human element we see: the massive, national grief, as nearly every household suffers some sudden death by supernatural cause. Yet the Lord does not cast it as a punishment on the people of Egypt but rather on the gods of Egypt. It suggests a larger principle: that to align oneself with the enemy of God is to be defeated along with that enemy.

Finally, we observe God's intention that "this day shall be a day of remembrance for you" and his instruction that "throughout your generations you shall observe it as a perpetual ordinance." These Old Testament themes of "remembrance" and future observances of the meal are surely recalled by Jesus' Last Supper words: "Do this, as often as you drink it, in remembrance of me" (1 Corinthians 11:25).

1 Corinthians 11:23-26

The long table began back in Egypt in the days of Moses. As we fast forward through the generations — past Joshua (Joshua 5:10), past Hezekiah (2 Chronicles 30:1-26), past Josiah (2 Kings 23:21-23; 2 Chronicles 35:1-19), and past Jerusalem of the Persian era (Ezra 6:19-22) — we come eventually to Jesus and his disciples. That spot on our table is the focus of our next lection.

Move your eyes just a little further down the table, however, and you come to the Corinthians of Paul's day.

Those first-century Greeks may seem far removed from us in terms of time and space, but the fact is that we may think of ourselves sitting right next to them at this table. In broad strokes, you see, their context is identical to ours.

Paul was writing to a congregation of Christians about their celebration of the Lord's Supper. That's what this table had become, even just a few decades after Jesus' Last Supper with his disciples on that Thursday night of Holy Week. Paul wanted to help that Christian congregation understand what they were doing.

As we read the larger context, we discover that not everything is copasetic in the Corinthian church. They are struggling with a variety of issues — divisions, infighting, immorality, to name a few — and unsurprisingly their worship and fellowship had been compromised. An unhappy family is not likely to have a cheerful dinner table just because they all agreed to sit down to eat together. Likewise, a troubled church will bring its troubles, one way or another, to this table of the Lord, as well. Accordingly, Paul wrote to help correct the problems in Corinth, including their mishandling of this meal.

In the course of his instructions, he includes these verses, which read to us more like a gospel than an epistle. And, indeed, he is functioning very much like a gospel writer, as he reports and records a piece of the narrative from Jesus' life.

The detail about Jesus giving thanks gives rise to the traditional term "Eucharist" for this meal. Meanwhile, for all of the elements that were likely a part of the disciples' Passover meal, it is just these two elements — the bread and the cup — that Jesus singled out as representative of him. The reference to a "new covenant" echoes Luke's account (22:20) and forms part of an important thread throughout scripture (Jeremiah 31:31; 2 Corinthians 3:5-6; Hebrews 8:8-13, 9:15, 12:22-24).

Jesus' instructions to "do this in remembrance of me" anticipate a continuing practice on the part of his followers. It is that practice in which Paul's congregation was participating. And it is at that table we sit next to them tonight.

41

This is the part of the table to which our eyes naturally turn on this holy day. Indeed, some of our people may not even know how much further back in time this particular table extends. But the narrator alludes to that history as he sets the stage with the reference to "the festival of the Passover." Still, Maundy Thursday is primarily about this moment in time, this part of the table, Jesus' Last Supper with his disciples.

John's gospel gives us a different view of this scene than Matthew, Mark, and Luke. That's not surprising, of course, because John gives us a very different view of most everything about Jesus' life and ministry than the synoptic gospels do. For starters, John's account of the Last Supper is several times longer than any of the other gospel records. We observe that two of the elements that are unique to John's Last Supper scene are found here in our selected verses: the foot washing and the new commandment.

Most of our congregations are unaccustomed to the practice of foot washing. While many folks who have tried it in various church settings have found it deeply meaningful, the fact is that the whole experience is a new and self-conscious one for most Americans. Consequently, we do not begin at the same starting place as Peter and the other disciples.

For those men around that table, foot washing was not a novel experience. Rather, in that world of dusty roads and sandaled feet, it was common practice. The mere experience of having another person wash one's feet, therefore, was not as awkward and uncomfortable for them as it is for us.

The experience of having Jesus wash their feet, however, was quite a different matter. That culture had a strong sense of hierarchy, and washing feet was servant's work. Jesus, however, was one whom they identified with titles like "master" and "lord." For them, he was at the other end of the spectrum from "servant." This is like having your boss come over for dinner only to roll up his sleeves and start cleaning your bathroom. This is the governor shining your shoes. This is the president washing and folding your laundry.

It was understandable, therefore, as well as personally typical that Peter would object. First, it seemed to him too backward that his lord should wash his feet. Then it seemed too little that only his feet should be washed. But Jesus walked his most mercurial follower through the logic and significance of the act. Then, when it was completed, he told his followers that the very inappropriateness of what he had done was precisely the point: "If I, your Lord and Teacher, have washed your feet, you also ought to wash one another's feet. For I have set you an example."

This symbolic act resonates with other teachings of Jesus (such as Matthew 20:20-28; 23:1-11; Mark 9:33-37). And whether or not our particular congregations are comfortable with the practice of washing one another's feet, the larger principle remains and must be applied: namely, that we are to live with the humble attitude of a servant. This is a high calling in the kingdom of God, and it is the posture we adopt before him and before one another.

Meanwhile, the "new commandment," which is another feature unique to John's Last Supper account, follows a similar trajectory. He commands his disciples to "love one another," which at first blush does not seem like a new commandment at all (cf. Matthew 22:37-40; Leviticus 19:18). But we discover that it is the standard for love that is new. No longer are we called to love "as you love yourself," but rather "just as I have loved you."

So the love commandment matches the message of the foot washing. That is to say, in both our serving and our loving, we are following Jesus' lead. As he has set an example for us, so we adopt an attitude of servitude with one another. And as he has loved us, so we love one another.

Imagine the church where these simple principles prevailed and became reality! Imagine the congregation where each one sought to serve the other and to selflessly love one another! By this, indeed, everyone surely would recognize that we really are his disciples!

Application

We come to a table on Maundy Thursday. Your table might look quite different from mine, of course.

Most of us will not literally have tables at all. As we kneel at the altar rail, file up and down the aisles, or even just remain in our seats with the elements of bread and cup brought to us, there's a table. And it's a very long table.

In order for our people to understand what we are doing together this evening, they need to see the whole table. So we begin with our ancestors who sat at the far end: Moses and his generation, hurriedly celebrating the first Passover meal together in Egypt. The meal marked God's saving act. Central to that saving act was the blood of a lamb. The meal was to be reenacted as a remembrance on that date throughout their generations.

After a good many generations had passed, Jesus and his companions sat down at that same table to eat, celebrate, and remember. Only now, suddenly, there was talk of different blood, and the anticipation of a different saving act. Again, there was the expectation that the meal would be reenacted as a remembrance throughout the generations.

So it was that, a few years later, the Christians in Corinth gathered at that table to eat, celebrate, and remember. And tonight we sidle up next to them, hearing again the story of "the night when he was betrayed."

There's something sweet about the faces we see as we look up and down this table. From the weathered skin of those Hebrew slaves in Egypt to that beloved collection of fishermen and more that gathered in that upper room; plus every imaginable look, size, complexion, and language that has appeared at this table in the generations since.

Then there is the sweetest face of all. He sits at the center of the table, and he is the host. As Charles Wesley sang, "Let every soul be Jesus' guest." He is the one who really brings us together, for it is because of his love and by his saving act that we are gathered here. He is the one we remember tonight. He is the greatest common factor among that widely disparate group represented across the generations and continents at this table. This meal is all about him.

Our host is the Paschal Lamb anticipated by Moses, the rabbi followed by Peter, the Savior proclaimed by Paul, and the Lord worshiped by us. We gather in his name, and we partake of his body and blood. We remember his saving act, we celebrate our salvation, and we proclaim his death until he comes.

An Alternative Application

Exodus 12:1-4 (5-10) 11-14; 1 Corinthians 11:23-26. "The act of remembering." Some of the remembering we do is deliberate. Some of it is inspired. Some of it is accidental. Of course, sometimes we don't remember, at all: we just plain forget.

Accidental remembering is that sort of experience in which some experience has the unintended effect of triggering a memory. I drive by a car with a Connecticut license plate, and I suddenly remember that my brother-in-law who lives in Connecticut has a birthday coming up. There is no design involved — except for the occasions when the design may be God's providence. It is just how the human brain works.

Inspired remembering is more like nostalgia. It is prompted by some smell, song, picture, group of friends, or what have you. You are inspired to indulge your memory in the fond exercise of reminiscing. It is like a floral centerpiece on the kitchen table: it has no real practical purpose, it's just a bit of loveliness.

Deliberate remembering is what we do most often. Specifically, it is what we do with the things we cannot afford to forget. With our alarms and alerts, our lists and notes to ourselves, our calendars and address books, we take deliberate steps to remind ourselves about those things we must not forget.

Deliberate remembering is what God had in mind for his people. There are certain things — big things — that we must not forget. So he built into his people's calendar the holy days and festivals that would prompt them to remember the truly important stuff.

We may think of "remembering" as a passive thing, and the phrase "in remembrance," which graces so many of our altars and Communion tables, sounds almost funereal to us. Yet biblical remembering is alive and active.

Whenever the scripture tells us that God remembered someone or something, it is followed immediately by action (Genesis 8:1, 19:29, 30:22; Exodus 2:24; 1 Samuel 1:19; Revelation 16:19). Naturally, therefore, when God commands his people to remember something (e.g., Exodus 20:8), appropriate corresponding action is expected.

Even the remembering itself is an action in God's design. The Old Testament Israelites were not merely instructed to pause once a year and recall God's saving action for their ancestors. No, they were to eat a meal and observe a festival, for participating in those actions would be full of remembering for them.

As we gather this evening to share the Lord's Supper together, we do so "in remembrance." It is to be "a day of remembrance for you," just as the Passover was for Israel. Our remembering will be active, not passive. And once we have remembered his atoning sacrifice, some corresponding action on our part would be appropriate.

T.O. Chisholm had a sense for what our corresponding action ought to be. "O Jesus, Lord and Savior," he sang, "I give myself to thee; for thou, in thy atonement, didst give thyself for me."

Good Friday
Isaiah 52:13—53:12
Hebrews 10:16-25
John 18:1—19:42
by Wayne Brouwer

Why did Jesus have to die?

While Don Richardson was a student at Prairie Bible Institute in the 1950s his heart burned in anticipation of bringing the good news about Jesus to an unreached tribe. He and Carol found their prayers answered in 1962 as they sailed out of Vancouver harbor toward Netherlands New Guinea. Before long they were deposited by missionary plane among the Sawi people, a group of tribes living in the trees of the interior rain forest.

The jungle floor was too damp for permanent dwellings, so the Sawi helped Don and Carol, and their infant son, Stephen, build a tree house in their neighborhood. Carol learned the ways of the Sawi women while Don spent time with the men, attempting to understand their language and reduce it to writing. Afternoons would find the Sawi males in one of their treetop workrooms, buzzing in conversation while they mended nets and hunting equipment, and swapped stories of fish and boars.

It was in this setting that Don took his first furtive steps toward speaking the Sawi language and reciting stories from the gospels. Most of the time the others ignored him, caught up in their own manly concerns. So the months progressed, with little Stephen becoming a Sawi child, Carol adapting meals to local produce, and Don attempting to get the message of the Bible into a form the Sawi could understand.

One day everything changed. Don was moving along in the gospel story to the last weeks of Jesus' life. As he related the tales about Jesus heading toward Jerusalem and the conspiracies that were swirling about him, the Sawi men began to listen. At first it was only that their conversations with one another died down, while their hands continued in busywork with their hunting and fishing tools. But then even this work ceased, and every eye was fixed on Don. He happened to be talking about Judas' secret meetings with the religious leaders and the betrayal that ensued.

Suddenly there was a murmur of approval and the delighted smiles of those who seemed to know this story. Don asked his translating helper what was going on. The reply chilled him to the bone, even in the heat of the tropics.

The Sawi, he was told, prided themselves for their hunting and fishing prowess. There was an even greater expression of manhood. They called it "Fattening the Pig for the Slaughter." It happened when one young man chose to target another young man in this or a neighboring clan and built a strong web of friendship. The two would hunt together and fish together and roam the forests together and eat together and laugh and talk together. They became best buddies. Then, when the relationship was secure, the initiator of the friendship would invite his comrade over to his mother's home for a grand meal. During the middle of the feast, when laughter was the language of the hour, and back-slapping good humor seasoned the supper, the first young man would suddenly pull out a long knife, brandish it with delight before the other's face, and when looks of dawning horror increasingly webbed out from the betrayed's eyes, plunge it through his "friend's" chest, piercing his heart.

The mother would come quickly with freshly baked bread that the traitor touched to his dead comrade's genitals before eating it. Then mother and son would open the skull of the victim, scoop out his brains, and consume these as well.

The deadly project was complete: one brave young Sawi warrior had displayed his cunning prowess and then had ingested all the power of his target. He became a greater man by taking into himself the strength and energy of his betrayed friend.

Don was dumbstruck! How could he communicate the story of Jesus and the love of God to these people if they viewed Judas, the betrayer, as the hero of the tale? Just as important, what was on the tribal menu for supper tonight? Were the Richardsons the next victims of "Fattening the Pig for the Slaughter"? Don slipped out of the men's lodge a wary and troubled man.

The story has a wonderful ending that will come at the conclusion of this article. But the central issue for Don and Carol Richardson is one that is key to all that Christians talk about and "celebrate" this week and this day: Why did Jesus have to die? Is his demise at a young age a symbol of weakness rather than strength? Is Christianity a religion of wimps who pride themselves in following the loser rather than the winner? How do you preach Christ on another Good Friday in a world that thrives on war, one-up-manship, devious politics, profits at all costs, and survival of the fittest in a cosmic game where the rules are heralded every Thursday evening: "Outwit, Outlast, Outplay!"?

Isaiah 52:13—53:12

Three major families of atonement theory have been proposed over the centuries to answer such questions. The first is linked to Isaiah's prophetic impressions in today's passage. God has been wronged. God's people have gone the way of wickedness and wastrels. The world is imbalanced and the Creator isolated from the people who are to him like loved but wayward children.

How will things be made right? Who will bring restoration and renewal and reconciliation? According to the word of the Lord through Isaiah, it will happen when "my servant" enters the picture and rewrites history. It is not clear exactly what the Suffering Servant will do, but the outcome is certain. After what appears to be a lackluster residential sojourn, those around the servant will attack him and cause him pain and kill him cruelly. But when all of that has happened, there will be a new peace between God and humanity and the former times of alienation will be gone.

Anselm interpreted this as Jesus' mission into our world to defend the honor of the Father. Because of the arrogance of spreading sin and the hubris of human communities that took the image of God, which they possessed for rebellious license, the Creator had been shuttered away from the creation, and Yahweh was forgotten except as a curse word.

But along came Jesus. Like one who still remembers the true nature of reality and appearing in the guise of a humble but faithful servant, Jesus takes up the thankless chivalric duty to restore the honor of the king of the castle, the lord of the estate. The Father might have been ready to wipe out the whole of humanity, just as Yahweh had threatened to Moses in Exodus 33, but then he saw the face of the Suffering Servant and realized that one still held him in honor. The faithful obedience of the one mitigated the divine wrath of God for the many and life on planet earth was restored and balanced.

Calvin took Anselm's ideas a step further, paying close attention to the forensic language of Paul in Romans and Galatians. It was not merely God's honor that had been violated, he said, but the righteousness of God's justice. We humans were not just rebellious clods, we had become downright guilty lawbreakers. Before the court of heaven none could stand with either pride or dignity. The eternal codes of propriety accused every person of failure, transgression, and fault.

Enter Jesus. Jesus comes as the lawyer for the accused. He does not pretend we are innocent but openly marks our guilt. Yet when the holy sentence is passed and capital punishment is ascribed against us, Jesus shows the extent to which he will advocate on our behalf. He himself steps into the penalty box, he himself climbs up to the gallows, he himself is strapped into the electric chair, he himself receives our toxic chemical cocktail and dies our death for us. There is good news about resurrection to come on Easter morning, of course, just as Isaiah hints at in the closing notes of his lament. But on Good Friday, the good news is that of escape and substitution.

Hebrews 10:16-25

A second family of atonement theories connects well with the book of Hebrews. It is not the Creator/Father who needs to take note of Jesus in his sufferings, but we humans. We have forgotten who we are. It may well be that we have offended God, but God is big enough to be able to handle it. What is more important is that we have offended ourselves. We have lost touch with our place in the house of God. We need a high priest who can help us find our way back home.

Jesus does this in a variety of ways. Irenaeus thought that Jesus had to be at least fifty years old when he died, because the point of Jesus' coming to earth was to go through all the stages of human life (fifty was certainly old age at the time!) in order to show us how to live and die correctly. We had lost our way. Only when we saw Jesus living our lives out of grace and love and courage, and even dying well, would we be able to do the same. He called Jesus' work "recapitulation," a replaying of human identity done right. What we observe most of Jesus on this Good Friday is his ability to die with courage and dignity, just as he had lived. When we see Jesus we buck up, get our acts together, and recover the best of our humanity.

Later theologians would further emphasize that exemplary character of Jesus' life and death. Abelard saw in Jesus' death the power of moral influence. We have grown complacent in our degradation, according to Abelard. Jesus comes among us and all we can see is his goody-goody character, and we despise him for it. We taunt him, trying to make him become a normal sinner like the rest of us. We tease him as if he were sub-human. When he refuses to play our dirty games we get angry with him and plot to get rid of him and ultimately throw him up on a cross in despicable shame. Only when the dastardly deed is done, it is not he but we who are suddenly cut to the heart. We hear his words from the cross, "Father, forgive them, for they know not what they do!" and we are embarrassed beyond loss of face. We see in his reflection what we have become and come to know the ugliness of ourselves for the first time. His morality pierces our immorality and we must turn away. Like the dirty, old man in one of O. Henry's stories, the one who sees by lamplight the beautiful woman he once called friend, but lost because of the blackness of his own rotten character and suddenly remembers what he could have been if he had stayed with her instead of becoming his awful self, we turn with him down a dark alley and bang our heads against a wall and cry out, "Oh God, what have I become?" Still in Jesus' love we find ourselves anew for the first time.

Schleiermacher and Ritchl would take up the same sermon generations later, preaching a morality in Jesus that becomes an example for us. Jesus' death was not a failure, but the ultimate testimony of love. Did not Jesus himself declare it? "Greater love has no one than this, that a man lay down his life for his friends!" Here is Jesus on the cross, condemned by the political powers of the day for combating power with love. While all of his troupe could have been sentenced and killed, Jesus was willing to stand alone, allowing the others to scurry off to save their skins. When they later realized what Jesus had done, they gained new courage to be like Jesus as well and formed a socially transforming movement that has since spanned the globe. "Be like Jesus!" they declare.

This is the kind of courage that comes in the final paragraph of our New Testament passage today. See what Jesus did and then live and die in similar fashion, for the good of the world.

John 18:1—19:42

There is also a third approach to atonement theory, and our gospel reading connects with it. For John, God's good world has been plunged into darkness by the viral effects of sin. Creation's brightness has been swallowed up by the shades of evil. Those who were made in the image of God have become ruined, warped, and distorted. It is the scene of Mordred in Tolkien's Middle Earth, where everything once righteous and holy has become twisted, perverted, distressed, and rotten.

All power appears to be in the hands of the Evil One, the "Father of Lies" as Jesus terms him in John 8:42-47. No relief from the shadows seems possible (note the place from which Nicodemus emerges in chapter 3 and the arena to which Judas exits in chapter 13) until Jesus calmly steps into the chasm manufactured by iniquity and it closes around him.

Origen called it a ransom to the devil. Satan, he said, was the greatest fisherman of all times, snagging every flippin' creature from the waters of this world. When his boat was filled to the limit, he headed for shore and a ravenous meal of consumption that would send us to his infernal bowels forever. Like any good fisherman, the devil snaked a troll line into the boat's wake on the journey back to harbor. Suddenly the reel whizzed out in a furious tug. A giant fish had gone for the devil's spinning lure!

Satan stopped rowing and fought the line. The fish at the other end was huge beyond belief. After playing it with practiced dexterity, the devil finally saw the fish near the gunwales. It was enormous! More than that, it was the Creator's own first creation! It was the Son of God!

Now the devil was in a dilemma. He did not have room for the big fish in his boat. He could keep either his current catch or toss it aside and claim the prize of the day, but he couldn't do both. Like any great fisherman, he chose the record breaker. Shoveling the little fish out of the boat, he managed to tease, taunt, and gaff the big one over the edge and get it to flop heavily onto the deck. His catch would be the news of heaven and earth!

As he wrestled his over-committed craft toward the docks, the trophy fish he prized gave a sudden wallop of its mighty tail, capsizing the boat and escaping into the water. In an instant the devil was left with nothing.

So, said Origen, is the story of Good Friday, when Satan, the prince of the powers of this age, played his biggest hand, trading all of wicked humankind for the big prize of God's own Son, and lost everything in the bargain. Why did Jesus have to die? Because it was the only way to get the rest of us free.

There is much of this in John's telling of Jesus' death. Everyone evil wants a piece of the action. Still Jesus himself is in charge of his own existence. On Easter morning, as we shall soon see, the big fish gets away, as do all of us who swim after him in the waters of baptism.

Application

The story of Jesus' horrible death is as familiar as it is enigmatic. We know that Jesus died and did so in a cruelly painful way but the why of it still remains fuzzy. Did Jesus have to satisfy God's honor or justice? Yes, that is indeed a message of the New Testament. Was his death an example to us and an act of moral persuasion? Certainly, for Jesus' own words testified to that. Were the evil powers that have locked their claws into this good creation of God weakened and perhaps ultimately destroyed in Jesus' infamous demise? That, too, is an element of the tale. But all are mixed together in ways that refute easy dissection or quick categorization.

Don and Carol Richardson survived their Sawi sojourn and even succeeded in bringing the gospel to these people. The story begun above took a later strange turn. Due to increasing scarcity, the Sawi people needed to range further in hunting and fishing. This, in turn, caused them to run into conflict with other area tribes and peoples. Soon there were skirmishes and fights and all-out wars. People returned to Sawi homes bloodied, battered, or missing limbs. Sometimes they failed to return at all, claimed by assassins' wounds and swallowed up by the putrefying womb of the jungle.

It was then that the men began to talk openly about the possible need for a "Peace Child." Intrigued, Don asked what they meant by that term.

Sometimes, they said, when war got too pronounced and murderous, when tribes were in danger of killing one another off, when brutality bested their will to live, one of the chiefs might grab the youngest newborn male baby from its mother's arms, and run swiftly, despite the woman's wailing, across the no-man's-land between the tribes. Reaching the first enemy village, he would thrust the baby into the arms of a young woman.

All knew what this meant. A son from one child was now the possession of the other tribe. Both tribes had a stake in the child's future and all warfare would cease for as long as that child lives. The "Peace Child" reconciled the foes.

Interest mounting, Don asked a further question. What would happen, he queried, if someone should kill the "Peace Child"? Horrified, the group shook their heads aghast. No one would ever think to do such a dastardly deed. It was beyond belief!

Hmmmm… thought Don. Then he proceeded. "Let me tell you a story…" he said. He related a tale of a time when the tribes of heaven and earth were at war with one another. He told of the chief of heaven bringing his own Son across the no-man's-land into our tribe as a "Peace Child." He explained how one day someone had instigated the murder of that "Peace Child." When the horrified Sawi warriors begged him about what could be done to erase this monumental human blunder, Don preached Christ and grace and the forgiving love of God.

An Alternative Application
John 18:1—19:42. The gospel story needs to be read today even if it is not preached. But if it is preached, and the approach above is taken, one of the greatest endings to the message would be a powerful recital of the dark night in C.S. Lewis' *The Lion, the Witch and the Wardrobe* in which Aslan is slain in the place of Edmund, but the magic from before time prevents the White Witch and her evil brood from winning the day. Declare the victory of Aslan with all the splendor of great drama.

Breaking boxes

The central message of Christian faith is that Jesus was raised from the dead. It is what sets apart Christianity from all other religions. As a teacher, Jesus was very good, but there were others who were also keen. As a prophet, Jesus was a tremendous cultural critic, but others also blasted the powers that ruled. As a miracle worker, Jesus was captivating, but so, too, have been many who pulled novel tricks. Yet when it comes to Easter, Jesus is unparalleled. No one else died and came back to life. In his resurrection Jesus proclaimed the dawn of a new age. The ultimate threat to human existence had been overcome. Jesus is alive and lives forevermore!

Today is a good day for some religious swaggering. We boast so easily about the little things of life: a winning sports team, a new car, and a birthday celebration. But the really big thing of life is our main focus today: Jesus came back from the dead and changed our thinking about life forever! We need to make this known and not hide it in tedium or ordinariness. Today is a good day for shouting and dancing a little! (See Paul's encouragement to boast in 1 Corinthians 1:31 — "Let him who boasts, boast in the Lord!")

For many years our family lived in Canada, and while there we adopted an expanded calendar of social holidays. Along with the usual Christmas and Easter, the shifted Thanksgiving and National Days, came the extra Canadian public festivities of "Civic Day" in August and "Boxing Day" on December 26. "Boxing Day" moved to Canada from England, where it began its career hundreds of years ago as the day on which the excesses of Christmas food were boxed up and distributed to the poor. More recently it has taken on the connotations of a time when the boxes and Christmas wrappings are smashed and trashed and discarded as unwanted leftovers from Christmas gift giving. After the thing of value has emerged from the box, the box is no longer needed. Such boxes need to be broken and made irrelevant. That idea fits with today's Easter preaching.

The three passages of today's lectionary all focus on breaking boxes, not literally, but metaphorically and theologically. When Peter preaches the good news of Jesus to Cornelius, he is breaking the box of ethnic separation that previously bound him, and also the box of religious understandings that had trapped both him and Cornelius prior to this. Paul's commands in his letter to the Colossians call for us to break the boxes of human perception and perspective by stepping into the vantage point of another person — the resurrected and ascended Christ. In John's gospel, all of the time-honored boxes of funeral regimen are obliterated as Jesus emerges from the shattered box of his tomb.

A good setup for today might be to create some boxes that are labeled with various falsely held myths of our human past (such as the earth is flat, no one can run the mile in under four minutes, heavier-than-air ships will never fly, communication is limited to earshot or eyesight distance, and the like) and then to break these boxes as a visible illustration.

Acts 10:34-43

The book of Acts is shaped according to Jesus' command in 1:8. In successive ripples we see the expansion of the church in and beyond "Jerusalem," through "Judea and Samaria," and then reaching past Asia Minor and Europe to the "ends of the earth." Luke makes this movement obvious to us through five similar "progress reports" (6:7; 9:31; 12:24; 16:5; 19:20). Each brings to a conclusion a mission movement that is broader than the last: Jerusalem (2:1—6:7), Judea, and Samaria (6:8—9:31), bridging the way to Gentiles (9:32—12:24), Asia Minor (12:25—16:5), and Europe (16:6—19:20).

It is helpful to understand the above plan for the book of Acts in order to appreciate the significance of Peter's words to Cornelius. Prior to this time Peter, along with virtually all of the early Jewish Christians, understood Jesus' coming, power, and meaning, primarily in terms of Jewish messianic terms. Nearly all of the first preaching of the good news of Jesus' resurrection was brought to Jews in Palestine. Suddenly, however, Peter is divinely led (Acts 10:9-23) to tell the same message of current divine favor and future hope to a prominent Gentile leader. This is a moment of historic significance, for it returns global significance (see Genesis 12:1-3) to the Israelite religion that has been marginalized and localized since the Babylonian conquest. Peter's perspectives are broadened to see God's eternal plan for the recovery of all God's children, not merely the Jews.

In bringing this hope to Cornelius, Peter declares that the confirmation of God's good favor is the Easter message. Jesus' resurrection, according to Peter, has several implications. First, it is God's affirmation of Jesus' ministry (10:40). While there have been many great religious teachers, none have had this kind of divine commendation. One can ignore Jesus' teachings and healings only until one confronts the empty tomb and the post-resurrection appearances of Jesus among his friends. After Easter, no one can write Jesus out of the picture because God did not.

Second, the resurrection of Jesus confirmed the power of Jesus' perspectives and theology for his followers (10:41). Suddenly they had a new understanding of what God's kingdom was about. Suddenly they became aware of the lengths God would go to bring reconciliation between heaven and earth. Suddenly they were emboldened to speak with strangers everywhere about a message of absolute significance for everyone. No one can remain the same after attending the funeral of a dear friend, spending time in the cemetery where his body is buried, and then seeing the exploded tomb and talking with him alive again. Jesus' resurrection confirmed the validity of his life, his teachings, and his view of God's history.

Third, Jesus' resurrection confirmed the urgency of the gospel message (10:42). People may hear a great orator and walk away with little or no permanent response. They may see mighty acts of healing and be religiously entertained for a time. But Jesus' open grave announced a new era in human history, according to Peter, one in which the future broke into the present and stared us in the face. These are suddenly the last days and they demand a response from all people.

In bringing this message of Easter's good news to Cornelius, Peter was breaking boxes. He was breaking out of the box of Jewish ethnocentricity. While Jewish monotheism required full devotion of members of its race, it was benignly pluralistic when it came to other races and other religions. Jewish monotheism was neither evangelistic nor "exclusivistic." Those from other nations might come to and adopt the God of Judaism, but it was a choice they would freely make. If they did not, there was no clear Jewish theology of divine judgment against them. But Peter's new understanding of God's broadened concerns changed all that. The box of Jewish ethnocentricity no longer made sense. The God of Israelite past was still the God of all nations. Jesus' resurrection was not a Jewish matter but a human issue — all people will die, all must face their maker, all are in need of the divine favor expressed through Jesus.

Peter was also breaking the box of Old Testament centripetal missiology. In the days of ancient Israel, Canaan was the land of covenant promise. Israel was to be a blessing to all the nations of the earth but was to transmit that blessing from its location on the crossroads of society. Israel's unique geographical location — squeezed between the Mediterranean Sea and the great desert, with Africa, Europe, and Asia on its southern and northern contact points — meant that all trade routes, all communication lines, and all conquest strategies would eventually bring the nations of its world into its borders. This would allow its religiously defined culture to be observed by other nations with the hopes that they would be attracted and become proselytes to its covenant identity (see Psalm 87). In this new stage of missiology, ushered in by Jesus' resurrection and the divine vision that had driven him to connect with Cornelius, the centripetal attraction to Israel's place was being transformed into a centrifugal thrust into the world at large. The box that limited the good news of God's work in human history to Israel's borders was being blasted from within.

Finally, Peter was acknowledging that the box of the grave was no longer absolute. If Jesus broke out of the tomb, no grave is any longer "safe." We can no longer assume that making it through life is enough. We must also become concerned about life beyond life, or life of eternal consequence. This places more of a moral imperative on the choice we make during our lives. The boxes are broken and, like Humpty Dumpty's shell, cannot be repaired. We have entered a new world order because of Easter.

Colossians 3:1-4

Paul wrote this letter from prison in Rome around AD 60. He was waiting for his case to be heard by the emperor (see Acts 21-28). A former slave acquaintance named Onesimus found his way to Rome and ended up as a constant and "useful" companion to Paul (see Philemon). Now Paul was sending Onesimus back to his master Philemon, who lived near Colossae. Tychicus would be Onesimus' traveling companion (see Colossians 4:7-9), and with such mail-deliverers available, Paul decided to send a letter to the Colossian church as well.

The focus of Paul's letter to the Colossians was his address of the "heresy" hinted at in chapter 2. That aberrant teaching appears to have been an early form of Ebionism, which was prevalent among Jewish Christians and Gentile proselytes to Judaism who later became Christians. This view held that Jesus was certainly a prophet divinely affirmed by God, but that the strength of Jesus' teachings was his ability to keep the commands of the Torah. Christians ought to follow Jesus' lead and observe the cultic rituals of Jewish faith, including the accretions that had been added over the years.

Paul resoundingly denies the validity of this approach. Furthermore, he espouses a Christology that is not adoptionistic (like that of the Ebionites), but rather incarnationist. Jesus was not merely a good man who was "adopted" by God because of his faithful observance of laws and commands but is actually the fullness of deity itself (2:9).

Because of that, the "normal" understanding of life is not from earthbound human perspective but from the divine, creator view. Since Christians are to identify with Jesus, they ought not limit their understanding of him to the times of his earthly sojourn, but also travel with him post-Easter as he returned to his heavenly frame of reference. This is the instruction Paul gives in 3:1-4.

A wonderful image that can be used effectively with this passage takes its title from E.M. Forester's great novel, *A Room with a View*. Forrester described the Italian travels of Lucy Honeychurch (note the name!) with her chaperone, and their disappointment in a fashionable Florence hotel where their explicit reservations of rooms with "views" (such as the sculpted gardens and open countryside) cannot be honored. Lucy is given a room overlooking the courtyard where the drama of human life is played out. In the end, it is she, not her chaperone, who has the true room with a view. This is what Paul is describing in godly terms. Our limited perspectives on human life are really boxes in which we have isolated ourselves. Jesus' resurrection and heavenly perspective allows us to break out of the boxes in which we have trapped ourselves, and see things from God's broader and more realistic view.

John 20:1-18

John begins his gospel with a philosophic perspective that ties the meaning of Jesus to the creation of the world (John 1:1-13) and the unique revelation of God to Israel through the Shekinah glory light (John 1:14-18). Chapters 2-12 are rightly called "The Book of Signs" because, through seven "miraculous signs," the glory of Jesus as the incarnate deity is gradually revealed. Chapters 13-20 are often called "The Book of Glory" because Jesus completes his revelation of divine glory first in his on-going relationship with the church through the witness of his disciples (13-17), and then through his sacrificial death as the true Passover Lamb (18-19). Here, in chapter 20, Jesus' resurrection is told in both its historical and cosmological significance. First comes the historical eyewitness report of the tomb being opened and emptied (20:1-13). Then, in verses 14-18, a cosmological dimension is added. John has told us that the tomb was located in a "garden" (19:41); here Mary supposes that she sees the "gardener" (20:15). While this is an explanation of real-time events, it is also an interesting return to John's original "creation/re-creation" themes of chapter 1. God created a garden in which humankind would dwell. Humans fell out of touch with their creator/gardener who used to come and talk with them in the garden. Now Jesus (the true gardener) is found again by his own in the garden. John is certainly making a play on this theme. Even the idea that Mary is not to cling to Jesus in the garden (v. 17) is part of the play; Jesus' resurrection is only the first stage in the process of "re-creation," and Mary must not halt it at this point.

Once again, boxes are broken on Easter. First, there is the box of the tomb. What ought to have held Jesus secure in death is demolished by *life*. Second, the human perspective of Jesus merely as a human companion is broken from the inside out when Jesus' full resurrection glory is displayed. Here Jesus cannot be held by limited earthly contacts. A few verses later he cannot be boxed into mere prophetic identity but must be declared "Lord" and "God" by Thomas (20:28).

John wants us to know that Jesus' resurrection on Easter Sunday is a message that has both personal and cosmological significance. Those of us who have been trapped into lifelessness because of the death of friends and relatives, know the personal release that Jesus' return to life brings. And all of us who have felt the limiting boxes of a cause-and-effect world begin to see outside the box when Jesus brings us back into fellowship with our Creator who wants to walk with us in the garden once again.

Application

We are in the habit of making boxes and God is in the habit of breaking boxes. Adam and Eve got trapped in the shame of their sinful nakedness; God restored their dignity with clothing and promises (Genesis 3). Lot got caught in the demonic box of Sodom's sin; God smashed the box and brought them back to life (Genesis 18-19). Pharaoh thought he could stash Israel in a confined corner of his empire; God exploded the myth of Egyptian supremacy and released the people of promise to find their way to a land of their own (Exodus 1-24). When Sennacherib and his Assyrian armies had Hezekiah and God's people locked up in the box of Jerusalem; God erased the limits of siege, sending the entrappers home and releasing the captives (2 Kings 18-19). Even when Israel played the same game and thought it had God locked in the box of the temple (see Ezekiel 1-10), God refused to stay in the box.

Easter is a box-breaking event. Nothing seems more secure to us than the metal-clad coffins in which we place the bodies of our dead, and the cement secure vaults in which they are buried. But God is in the habit of breaking boxes, even those that seem incredibly secure, and Easter proves it once and for all. No box could hold Jesus. No trap of death could snare him. Easter is "Boxing Day," when the last great boxes that confine, outline, refine, define, and malign us are broken. So boast about it!

An Alternative Application
John 20:1-18. If you would like to focus only on the resurrection story in John, several themes emerge. First, John tells us that the events take place early in the morning, "while it was still dark." Light and darkness are very meaningful in John's gospel — in chapter 1, God creates the world full of light, but it becomes dark; Jesus is the light of God entering this dark world, and only those who see his glory become bearers of the light of God. In chapter 3, Nicodemus comes to Jesus at night, but is given a sendoff that surrounds him with light; in chapter 13, Judas enters the room of Jesus' farewell discourse surrounded by the light of Jesus' glory, but when challenged about his motives, leaves the room "and it is night." Here darkness is both the condition of the morning and the figurative blindness or uncertainty of those who do

not yet fully comprehend the significance of Jesus' resurrection.

Second, in John's description of the tomb there is evidence of resurrection that resoundingly speaks against grave robbery. Grave robbers would not unwrap a body at the grave; they would make sure they were in a safe place before doing so, but here the strips of linen that were used to wrap the body of Jesus appear to have fallen in place. This would not be so if Jesus' body were unwrapped from the outside; nor could it happen if the one wrapped had only fainted and then come back to life (remember how Jesus commanded others to unwrap Lazarus in John 11). At the same time, the headpiece was folded and placed off to the side by itself. John's testimony speaks of a body that miraculously passed through its death wraps, dropping them in place, and of a living human who took off his death skullcap, folded it and put it away because it was no longer needed.

Now it's time to preach

The Sunday after Easter is an unenviable time for preachers in many churches. The mood and events of Holy Week have both a depth and an excitement that can make the Sunday after Easter something of a letdown. The palm branches are gone. The lilies are gone, and it will seem that a great many people are gone too. Surely the attendance in so many of our American churches is a letdown on the Sunday after Easter.

So what shall we do on the Sunday after Easter? Take a vacation? Follow the lead of our people who stay home in great numbers this day? Bring in someone off the bench to fill the pulpit?

Throughout the gospels, Jesus repeatedly told people not to spread the word about him. After they were healed (Luke 5:14), after they witnessed miracles (Matthew 17:9; Mark 7:36; Luke 8:56), after they had discovered something of his identity (Matthew 16:20), he consistently admonished people not to tell anyone.

That gag order was not permanent, however. Jesus indicated as much when he was coming down from the mountain where he had been transfigured before Peter, James, and John. "Tell no one about the vision," he said, "until after the Son of Man has been raised from the dead" (Matthew 17:9). And therein lies the key for us. What are we to do after Easter? After he has been raised from the dead? Tell!

The gospel does not consist of his miracles, healings, teachings, or even identity. Only after he had been crucified and raised was there something to tell. So now, especially on the Sunday after Easter, it's time to preach.

Acts 2:14a, 22-32

We preachers feel considerable pressure to be relevant. The world in which we live does not widely cherish preaching. Indeed, in everyday idiomatic English, "preach" is a rather negative word. For example, "Don't preach at me!" and "I didn't mean to sound preachy." When you and I stand up to preach, we feel the need to say something that will be perceived and received as relevant to the folks in our congregation. "What does this have to do with me and my life?" is the relevancy litmus test.

In light of the contemporary demand for personal relevancy and immediate application, we may rightly be startled by Peter's sermon on Pentecost. In our excerpted passage, for example, the only real point of personal connection Peter makes with his audience is to refer to them as the ones to whom Jesus was handed over and by whom he was crucified.

I'm trying to imagine Peter distributing to the crowd at the beginning a little photocopied sermon guide with blanks to be filled in. "You see the line," Peter says, "that reads, 'God sent Jesus. God used Jesus. And we _____ Jesus'? Go ahead and write 'killed' in that blank."

That's more personal relevancy than we bargained for.

Peter does not suffer from any confusion, however, about the subject of his preaching. He preaches Christ. He preaches what Christ did, what the scriptures say about Christ, the people's culpability in not recognizing but rejecting Christ, God's act of raising Christ from the dead, and the witness of those who had known and seen Christ. He preaches Christ.

Sometimes the demand for relevancy tempts us to preach about current events but that may reflect a fallacious paradigm: one that we ought to help our people out of, rather than climbing into it ourselves. The paradigm assumes that "current" and "relevant" naturally go together. Our proclamation of the gospel, however, asserts two other things. First, that some very ancient events are relevant — indeed, more personally life-impacting than many or all current events. And, second, that these ancient events are, in fact, current, for the resurrection makes them so. Our gospel is not dead and buried in the past. Rather, we proclaim one who is risen and alive. He is, therefore, always current and his saving death and resurrection are always relevant.

In the end, Peter called upon the Pentecost congregation to repent, to be baptized in Jesus' name, and to receive the Holy Spirit. The gospel calls for personal response. It seems, therefore, that the preacher of the gospel does not need to seek some relevant message for the people. Rather, the preacher of the gospel implores the people to make the message personally relevant in their own lives.

1 Peter 1:3-9

Call it, "Theology on a Time Line." That's the style of this intricate opening paragraph from Peter's first epistle. Tightly woven together in just these few verses, Peter has expressed his understanding of the Christian's past, present, and future.

The past is the part least elaborated here, although he returns to that theme repeatedly in later portions of this epistle (see, for example, 1:14, 18; 2:9b-10; 4:3). Within the present passage, the past is summarized by the reference to the new birth that God has given us (v. 3).

The present, meanwhile, is a manifestly mixed bag. On the one hand, it is a time of testing and suffering. This is one of the recurring themes of Peter's letter — the problem of suffering was clearly a major issue for the Christians to whom Peter wrote. At the same time, however, the present is also a time of hope and rejoicing. It is a time lived under God's protection, and it is the time of "receiving the outcome of your faith, the salvation of your souls."

Finally, the future. The future is not at all a mixed bag. The future is all good. Paul piles up unalloyed adjectives to describe the inheritance that awaits us in God's good future. It is also anticipated as a time of "praise and glory and honor when Jesus Christ is revealed," and the implication is that the suffering will be past and we will finally and fully see the one in whom we have believed and whom we have loved.

Two broad points can be derived from these observations. First, there is the central role of God in past, present, and future. In our past, God gave us something — and that gift, of course, was predicated upon a great many things he did in the past! In the present, he protects, saves, and proves us. In the future, he marvelously fulfills all that he has in store for us and for the world.

We do not see any period of our lives clearly if we do not see God in the midst of it. We all ought to devise a kind of "time line theology" — and help our congregations do the same — by which we affirm the presence and providence of God in our past, present, and future.

Second, there is the relative influence of the past and the future on the present. We are more naturally conscious, of course, of how the past influences the present. We see the past more clearly, which makes its influence easier to trace. Also, our deeply ingrained sense of cause-and-effect gives perhaps disproportionate credit to the past for the present.

What comes after is the heir of what comes before, right? It cannot work the other way, can it? Can it be that what will come after gives birth to something in the present?

Precisely that phenomenon is very much a part of our common experience, and it is a part of Peter's testimony and teaching here. While organic cause-and-effect flows always from past to present, and from present to future, the tide of influence can flow the other direction in other areas of life.

It is the future prospect of college, not the past experience of middle school, that makes the high school student work hard in the present. It is the upcoming summer's swimsuits, not the past winter's sweaters and coats, that prompt us to diet in the present. "Effect" may be the past's heir. "Preparation," however, is the progeny of the future.

And so, as Peter lays out his theology on a time line, we are struck by this unavoidable conclusion: The Christian's life in the present is meant to be more a response to the future than to the past. Our joy, our hope, our confidence, our faithfulness, our peace — these are not traced back to what has gone before, and they are often very much in spite of what goes on now. We live toward a final destination rather than a point of origin. God's future is the greatest influence on our present.

John 20:19-31

Some biblical characters rightly deserve the negative reputations that they have: Jezebel, Nebuchadnezzar, Judas, and Pontius Pilate. Thomas, however, does not. He has an undeserved reputation.

We know a fair amount about a few of the disciples, for they play significant roles in the gospels and Acts, and perhaps wrote some of the New Testament epistles. Meanwhile, we know practically nothing about others among the twelve. They are just names on the list, but we don't have a record of anything that they individually said or wrote or did.

Then there is Thomas. We don't know much about him, for he does not figure prominently in the gospel stories or in Acts. Rather, what we know about him comes mostly from this passage from the gospel of John, and this episode has so fashioned our impression of him that his reputation has become an expression, his name has become a nickname — "doubting Thomas."

I suggest that Thomas has been wrongfully singled out from among the disciples, for they were no paragons of belief on Easter or even afterward.

When Mary and the other women first returned from the empty tomb with the good news, what was the response of the disciples? Did they begin singing alleluias? No, but rather the women's "words seemed to them an idle tale, and they did not believe them" (Luke 24:11). That's a remarkable statement, isn't it? Here we have no less than the apostles hearing nothing less than the gospel word that Jesus is risen, and they reject it as nonsense. We, as preachers, need never be discouraged by the slow, halfhearted, or incredulous response of a congregation. Our congregations are in good company, for the apostles themselves did not make much of an audience for the gospel on Easter Sunday.

Mark reports, meanwhile, that Jesus appeared to two disciples, but when they returned to tell the rest of the group, the others would not believe (Mark 16:13). Accordingly, after that event, when Jesus did appear to the disciples all together, Mark writes that "he upbraided them for their lack of faith and stubbornness, because they had not believed those who saw him after he had risen" (Mark 16:14).

Even at the penultimate moment in Matthew's gospel, just before Jesus ascends into heaven, the author reports of those gathered around Jesus: "When they saw him, they worshiped him; but some doubted" (Matthew 28:17). Well after Easter, after many experiences and exposures, still "some doubted."

Upon further review, therefore, we discover that Thomas does not deserve to be singled out. He is singled out in history only because he happened to be the one not there when all the others were. Let's not call him "doubting Thomas," therefore, just "absent Thomas," or "bad-timing Thomas," or some such. But his doubt is no more remarkable than any of the other disciples.

Honestly, we don't even need to travel beyond the confines of this pericope from John's gospel to vindicate Thomas. On the first occasion when the risen Christ appeared to his disciples — the time when Thomas was not present — see the order of events. Jesus appeared and greeted them. Did they respond with recognition and rejoicing right away? Not according to the story. Rather, "after he said this, [Jesus] showed them his hands and his side. Then the disciples rejoiced when they saw the Lord."

There's no evidence that Thomas was not more incredulous than the others, just perhaps more outspoken in his incredulity. And, of course, his outspokenness cuts the other way, for while the other disciples may rejoice in the risen Christ, none matches Thomas' testimony and Christology in the end: "My Lord and my God!"

Application

I was sitting in a meeting recently in one of our denominational offices. Within view, I could see an assortment of resources on the bookshelves: resources for pastors, churches, Sunday school classes, and so on. There were packages of curriculum, church-growth resources, assorted programs for different ages and stages of life, church advertising tools and kits — a whole range of products, some designed for folks within the church and others targeting people outside the church.

As I sat there, examining the materials from a distance, I was struck by a theme in the packaging. People's faces. On so many of the products: collages of faces, with a healthy diversity of age, gender, and ethnicity represented.

I know that packaging is about marketing, and I don't pretend to be an expert in that very sophisticated field, but the packaging I saw made me wonder just what it is that we are selling — or, more appropriately, what it is that we are offering.

I have a recollection from my childhood that there used to be within the church a real preponderance of pictures of Jesus. He was pictured on the covers of our children's Sunday school booklets. His picture was on mission bulletin boards, on classroom walls, on bulletin covers, and on adult curriculum materials.

Admittedly, our old pictures of Jesus had their problems. He was Caucasian, and he seemed to come from either North America or Western Europe. Nonetheless, he was pictured everywhere and on everything we did, and while that is not an achievement by itself, it perhaps offered a certain clarity of purpose and message.

The marketing was not nearly so slick back then, to be sure, with all of our mimeographed bulletins and newsletters, but the message of our packaging was clear. What we had to offer was Christ.

That's what you and I have to offer this week. As we continue to celebrate and affirm his resurrection, we preach Christ. Just as Peter preached Christ to the curious crowds in Jerusalem on Pentecost, Christ is our message to the congregations we serve. All three of this week's lections give us ample material to explore and declare, not just his resurrection, but his person and work.

The pictures on so much of our present packaging neglect the product. Let that not be said of our preaching. We ought not begin with the ones to whom we are preaching, but rather with the one about whom we are preaching. He is current and relevant all by himself. He suffers only — now, as with the doubting disciples, as with the crowds whom Peter addressed — from being unrecognized. Our preaching sets out to change that.

An Alternative Application

John 20:19-31. This passage is so full that its possibilities for preaching are nearly endless. We devoted most of our attention above to Thomas, and, in preaching the main suggested theme for the week, we might devote ourselves especially to Thomas' exclamation, "My Lord and my God!"

Verse 23 stands out even within this brimming passage, however, for it is a verse that gives pause to many Protestant Christians. If you have an appetite for preaching the hard sayings of Jesus, this Sunday's gospel lection offers you an opportunity.

If I were going to preach Jesus' word to his disciples in John 20:23, I would not begin there. I would begin, instead, with a story. Two stories, really, from the Old Testament and I would set them side by side.

The first story would be the tragic story of King Saul. Few characters in scripture are as sad as Saul. He has no particular ambition at the outset, yet greatness is thrust upon him. Then he mismanages it in such a disastrous way that, in the end, we see him disguising himself to visit a witch, falling on his own sword in battle, and having his weary corpse paraded and abused by the Philistines.

The second story would be the grand story of King David. Not only is his reign strong and majestic, the groundwork for Israel's golden age under Solomon, but his legacy is like no one else's in scripture.

His life becomes the standard by which subsequent kings in Jerusalem are measured. His reign becomes the symbol for the messianic reign and God's ultimate kingdom. From Jesus' birth in Bethlehem to his triumphant entry into Jerusalem, David is recognized as the key ancestor in Jesus' lineage, and David's star still flies on the flag over the modern state of Israel.

A side-by-side comparison of Saul and David, however, reveals two kings with significant failures. Indeed, upon further review, David's terrible episode with Bathsheba and Uriah seems much more marked by calculated wickedness than any of Saul's misdeeds, which smack more of weakness than willfulness. Yet Saul is tragic, while David is triumphant. Why?

I suggest that the difference between these two men is not so much in their performance as something else. I wonder if the difference between these two men — an immense difference, in the end — is partly attributable to the prophets who worked with them.

From the very suggestion that Israel was to have a human king, the prophet Samuel is offended by and opposed to the idea. His introduction of Saul seems to hamstring him from the start. And his in-person response to Saul's failures is harsh and unforgiving.

Nathan, by contrast, becomes an agent of grace in David's awful hour. He tells the famous story that touches the former shepherd's heart, he enables David's repentance, and he assures David of God's forgiveness.

I would juxtapose the stories of Saul and David, with special attention to the comparison of Samuel and Nathan. Then I would introduce Jesus' words: "If you forgive the sins of any, they are forgiven them; if you retain the sins of any, they are retained." It is not authority for the apostles; it is responsibility for Christ's followers. We may be instruments of condemnation or we may be agents of grace.

Read the manual

My friend was overwhelmed by his first church convention. "It's all so big," he wrote in his report. "There is so much going on. I wish I had a manual to instruct me on what to do, where to go, and how to vote."

Someone responded to his report with a letter to an editor. "How sad," said the letter, "that a leader of our church would not know that we Christians already have a manual on how to live the Christian life. It's called the Bible."

The letter writer was vastly unfair to my friend, who was asking for a manual to the convention, not to the faith. But the letter writer was also unfair to the Bible itself, which is far from a manual. It is not a set of instructions. It contains history, poetry, and fiction as well as instruction. It must be read in a complex dialogue with tradition and common sense. Much of it makes sense only in an ancient context and cannot easily be translated into a modern setting. (I defy anyone to come up with an adequate modern analogy to Paul's prohibition of eating meat offered to idols in 1 Corinthians 8-10.)

However, there are passages in the Bible where the "manual" analogy works on a small scale. We read three such passages today. Peter's sermon in Acts is a manual on how to live the resurrected life. The letter that goes under Peter's name addresses the same subject, and Luke, who is telling a story rather than writing a manual, still subtly manages to instruct us in how to live under a risen Lord.

Acts 2:14a, 36-41

Peter's long Pentecost speech is divided into several sections in the lectionary. Today we read his closer — this is where he asks for the signatures that would close the sale. To review the story: the twelve (and perhaps 120 disciples with them) have been filled with the Spirit and inspired to preach the risen Lord (2:1-4). This has drawn a crowd of Pentecost pilgrims to listen (2:5-13). Peter, as the leader of this group, stood to proclaim that these events proved that the last days predicted by the prophets were upon them; God was at work here (2:14-21). This gave Peter the opportunity to preach the gospel (2:22-36, the first of several summaries of early Christian preaching in Acts, which Luke notes is merely a *précis*, v. 40). The interaction with the crowd (2:37-42) will lead to an idealized portrait of the early community (2:43-47).

The heart of Peter's speech is the affirmation that the resurrection proves Jesus' true identity: "Therefore let the entire house of Israel know with certainty that God has made him both Lord and Messiah, this Jesus whom you crucified" (2:36). The issue of "certainty" is crucial to Luke's work; he has already told us that "certainty" is the purpose of his writing (Luke 1:4). Peter's listeners (and Luke's readers) can be certain that God is fulfilling the promises made to Abraham — because it's happening before their eyes! Luke reinforces the connection to the tradition by using the archaic-sounding "House of Israel," and by giving Jesus two traditional titles, "Lord" and "Messiah."

Peter's last words were pointed directly at the crowd ("this Jesus whom you crucified"), and as so often in Luke-Acts, his speech is interrupted at its climax. The emotional response of the hearers, "Brothers, what should we do?" is a sign of the Spirit's work (2:37). Peter's response is twofold: "Repent, and be baptized every one of you in the name of Jesus" (2:38). "Repent" indicates a complete change of life, a turning around to walk in the opposite direction. It is an especially poignant word on the lips of Peter, who knew what it meant to get a second chance — and now all Israel is given that second chance! Peter commends baptism (although there is no record of the twelve or even the 120 being baptized) "in the name of Jesus" (it is not clear whether this was an alternative to the trinitarian baptismal formula, or simply a recognition of the power and authority behind Peter's proclamation). The promised results are also twofold: "Your sins may be forgiven, and you will receive the gift of the Holy Spirit." Peter is using a financial image in the promise that sins will be forgiven, like a debt. His promise of the Spirit extends beyond those listening to his sermon, "For the promise is for you, for your children, and for all who are far away, everyone whom the Lord our God calls to him" (2:39).

Luke tallies the number of those who responded to Peter's challenge at 3,000 (he does not mention the mechanics of getting all those people baptized!). The large number indicates the magnitude of the growth: from a mere seed of 120, the community has grown nearly thirtyfold. This is the restored people of God, God's new work in Israel, the firstfruits of a new Pentecost.

1 Peter 1:17-23

What Luke did for the Jewish people, 1 Peter does for the Gentiles — trace the theological connection between God's act in raising Jesus from the dead to its practical benefit for those who believe. Peter lays out the whole system, step by step. It is truly a manual for the community of the resurrection.

The manual might be titled, "How to Be Holy." The instructions specify that holiness is God's work, not ours. Peter moves to his main theme almost as soon as he begins the body of the letter: "Be holy yourselves in all your conduct; for it is written, 'You shall be holy, for I am holy'" (1:15-16). Peter quotes from Leviticus 19:2, in full acknowledgment of the Hebrew notion of "holiness," which at root is "separation." God is "holy" in the sense of being "set apart" from all created things. The people of God are to be "holy" in that same sense — set apart and different from their pagan neighbors. Thus, Peter employs the metaphor of the "Diaspora" as our lection begins: "If you invoke as Father the one who judges all people impartially according to their deeds, live in reverent fear during the time of your exile" (v. 17). Like the Jewish Diaspora, Gentile Christians are to live as aliens and sojourners in a hostile land. Their lives and actions prove them to be different from others.

Peter grounds his instruction in some theological basics. God is judge; that is, God is the only one who sees human beings impartially, for who they really are and what they really do (v. 17). Further, the God who knows us truly has sacrificed for us; God is the one who has bought our freedom. Peter uses the image of the "ransomer," one who pays to free a slave (it was not unheard of for a philanthropist or temple to redeem and set free a slave; Peter pictures God doing this on a widespread scale, v. 18). Peter invokes Passover imagery when he speaks of "the precious blood of Christ" being "like that of a lamb without defect or blemish" (v. 19; cf. Exodus 12:5; Leviticus 22:21); his contrast of perishable/imperishable will carry over into his discussion of the power of God's word in 1:23.

The redeemer judge God was at work from the beginning in Christ, who was "destined before the foundation of the world" (v. 20). Fortunately for you, Peter says, "he was revealed at the end of the ages for your sake" (the parallel clauses are hymnlike). This is the same language he has already used to describe Christians (v. 2); there is an analogy between God's work in Christ and God's work in Christians. God's work included raising Christ from the dead and to glory, with the corresponding result of faith and hope among believers (v. 21). This is the new birth that comes through the word (v. 23).

The Christian life is the appropriate response to God's work in Christ on our behalf. Peter exhorts his readers to "live in fear" (the NRSV qualifies the "fear" as "reverent," v. 17). They are to turn "from the futile ways inherited from your ancestors" (v. 18). They are to trust in God (v. 21). This trust is variously specified as including faith, hope, obedience, and love (vv. 21-22; the NRSV's "genuine mutual love" is literally "brotherly love" within the community, a necessary commodity if, as many think, Peter was writing to a persecuted church, cf. 4:14, 16). Yet even these virtues are not human work, because they are guaranteed by God's work in Christ (v. 21). Christians are to live as purified souls (v. 22); again, this recalls the Passover lamb who by virtue of baptism has been "born anew" (v. 23).

Luke 24:13-35

Luke continues the textbook approach to the basics of the resurrection, this time in narrative form. In the Emmaus story, the disciples restate some basic Lukan themes. But Jesus himself fills in the blanks, explaining how these events have been a part of God's plan all along. In teaching the disciples the true meaning of his life, death, and resurrection, Jesus shows how they can come to recognize him on a regular basis in the breaking of the bread.

The Emmaus story is a bridge between the empty-tomb narrative and the appearance of the risen Lord to all the disciples. It touches on a number of important Lukan themes: the centrality of Jerusalem as the place of God's work, the revelation of Jesus in teaching and Eucharist, and the fulfillment of prophecy. It is a "recognition story" of a type common in both the Hebrew Bible and in Greco-Roman storytelling, where hospitality to a stranger pays off in unexpected ways. Most importantly, it puts Luke's readers back on the road, echoing Jesus' original trip to Jerusalem (9:51—19:27).

Emmaus was a short trip from Jerusalem (the exact location is uncertain). Luke identifies Cleopas and his unnamed companion as two of those who had heard yet disbelieved the women's story of an empty tomb (v. 13). These two were having an extended discussion on the meaning of the events of these last few days (v. 14). They were joined by Jesus himself, though "their eyes were kept from recognizing him" (Luke often uses the image of sight and vision as a metaphor for faith and salvation, cf. 1:78-79; 2:30; 4:18-19; 6:39-42; 10:23; 11:34; 18:35-42; 19:42). The defect here was not their comprehension of the things that had happened, but the lack of proper perspective, which only Jesus could provide. Their state of affairs is quite poignantly summed up by Luke in their response to Jesus' greeting: "They stood still, looking sad" (v. 17).

Cleopas recounts the story so far in quite Lukan terms. Jesus is described as the "Prophet like Moses," mighty in word and deed before God and the people (v. 19; cf. Deuteronomy 34:10-12). The response to this prophet was divided: the leaders of the people gave him over to condemnation and death (v. 20), but "we had hoped that he was the one to redeem Israel" (v. 21). The empty tomb story is recounted with some astonishment, but inconclusively, as if the simple fact of its emptiness was not enough to evoke faith in them (vv. 22-24).

Jesus' response is that of a prophet: "Oh, how foolish you are, and how slow of heart to believe all that the prophets have declared!" (v. 25). Of course, what they lack is a proper messianic understanding of the scriptures, and who better to provide it than the Messiah himself? Luke shows the church how to read scripture in this passage: the Hebrew Bible must be read through and by Jesus. It points to him as it details the prophetic pattern he followed: rejection, suffering, death, and vindication. "Was it not necessary that the Messiah should suffer these things and then enter into his glory?" (v. 26).

Luke gives us a recognition scene with a bit of playful suspense, as Jesus threatens to walk off anonymously into the sunset (vv. 28-29). Instead, he accepts the hospitality offered by the two disciples and proceeds to recall his actions at both the miraculous feeding and the Last Supper: he took, blessed, broke, and gave bread (v. 30). Like innumerable Christians since then, their eyes were finally opened, and he was "made known to them in the breaking of the bread" (v. 35). Retrospectively, they understood how he was also made known in the messianic teaching from the scriptures: "Were not our hearts burning within us while he was talking to us on the road, while he was opening the scriptures to us?" (v. 32).

The two return immediately to report to the others. Their report is almost pre-empted with the announcement that greets them: "The Lord has risen indeed, and he has appeared to Simon!" Nevertheless, the two disciples fulfill their duty and become types of the faithful Christian, who not only meet Jesus in the scriptures and the breaking of the bread, but also witness their experience to all who will hear.

Application

I once was working with a church that wanted to do evangelism. "Here's an idea," someone said, "let's get the listings of all the new housing purchases in the area, and we'll make up a flyer and send it out to the new people who move in. We'll be like the Welcome Wagon."

It was not a bad idea in and of itself, publicity-wise, but as a sole plan of evangelism, it had a few flaws (a good response on that kind of mailing would be about one percent). I tried to reason with them.

This was a small church, average attendance less than 100. "What's the most important thing about this church?" I asked, "What makes you come back each week?"

"We're like a family," they kept saying, "We treat each other like a family."

"What does it mean to be a family?"

"You live together," they said, "you eat together, you work together, and you have fun together."

"How do you bring new members into a family?"

That one stumped them.

"Well," I said, "you either get born into it or adopted. Now say you're going to adopt a child — how are you going to find a child to adopt?"

That stumped them too. If only there were an adoption agency for potential new church members; we could just drop by on Sunday morning and pick up a few.

"One thing's for sure," I told that group, "you're not going to invite new members into your family by sending out mass mailings. You wouldn't even send out a flyer to get guests for a dinner party. In a family, you want people not only to eat with you, but live with you, work with you, and play with you. How can you expect to invite people to join your family without a personal invitation?"

Jesus has given us a handbook on how to bring our friends and neighbors to him. First, we need to understand the scriptures. Next, we need to understand theology. Then we need to understand how those two things connect to our everyday lives — we need to repent, be baptized, be born anew, learn from Jesus, and see him in the stranger and in the community. In short, we need to live the Christian life ourselves.

Then we can invite people into the family, personally.

Alternative Applications

1) Luke 24:13-35. Preachers need to keep alert to the dark side of scripture, even in its brightest moments. One prominent problem in recounting the passion narratives is the polemic edge of all the gospels, which could easily be twisted into anti-Semitism, in the form of "the Jews killed Jesus." Good teaching is an effective antidote to that sort of nonsense. In Luke's case, clearly it is not "the Jews" but a subset of a divided Jewish people who is held responsible for the betrayal of Jesus. Cleopas' speech in Luke makes the division clear: The leaders of the people handed him over to be condemned to death and crucified him (and even here, Cleopas is stretching it — only Romans had the power to crucify). As for the common people, they tended to respond positively to Jesus, according to Luke. The theme of division is Luke's way of addressing a fundamental theological question for his community: Why, if Jesus is the promised Messiah, did not all the Jewish people believe in him? Luke's answer is that some did, some didn't — the people were divided, with the leaders going against Jesus. He is not writing history so much as an explanation of how the church came to be dominated by Gentiles. He certainly would have been appalled to find anyone using his work to justify hatred against the Jewish people.

2) 1 Peter 1:17-23. In their book, *Resident Aliens: Life in the Christian Colony* (1989), Stanley Hauerwas and William H. Willimon challenged mainline Christians to rethink their role in contemporary society.

Christendom, the American fusion of state and civil religion, according to Hauerwas and Willimon, is dead. And that, they think, is a good thing! The Christian faith cannot be institutionalized into an unofficial state religion without being distorted into something it is not. True Christianity absent Christendom can now live on as if in a Diaspora, an enclave separate from a society that challenges and provokes the values of that society. We are to be "resident aliens," no longer trying to accommodate our beliefs to the norms of society, but speaking out and living out a vision of faith that sees Christ's self-giving as its norm. Gone will be the appeal to selfish and self-serving religious "needs" in favor of a genuine commitment to the God revealed in Jesus Christ. In the terms used by the author of 1 Peter, we will "live in reverent fear during the time of our exile."

by Wayne Brouwer

Finding safety in the call of the wild

There are two themes that run through the passages for today. On the one hand there is the "Call of the Wild" (like Jack London's 1903 novel), in which we are commanded to follow our Shepherd Jesus through what might be trackless wastes and difficult places in responding to the great challenge of faith. On the other hand, there is the "Call of the Safe" (like Larry Crabb's great book on small groups, *The Safest Place on Earth* [Word, 1999]), which places us in the middle of a community of care and grace.

George MacDonald helps us understand both of these homing calls in his children's tale, "Papa's Story." Papa tells of a shepherd who brings his flock home late on a stormy evening. One lamb is missing, however. So, after supper, the shepherd calls for Jumper the dog and the two of them brace for the cold and wind and rain. Out in the hills they roam, calling for the wee lamb.

Young Nellie is snug in her bed at home but every moaning of the breeze echoes with her father's distant voice. She is frightened for him, for Jumper, and for the little lamb they seek. Suddenly, father is home, and Jumper too! They have found the little lamb and have returned it to safety in the fold. The tests of the night have taken their toll on father. How weary he looks, and how torn, cut, dirty, and bleeding is Jumper!

When little Nellie returns to bed, she dreams that *she* is Jumper and that the little lamb is her lost brother Willie. A year earlier, young Willie left home. He wanted to get away. Now Willie lives in Edinburgh and never writes. Nellie and her parents know from the scuttlebutt of traders and friends that Willie has become only a shadow of himself, cruel and greedy, filthy of body and mind, constantly drunk and lost in a mad world of sex.

In Nellie's dream she is Jumper, searching through the storms of Edinburgh's wilder haunts for the little lamb with Willie's face. When she wakes the next morning, Nellie acts on her dream and goes to find her brother. After hours of struggle and pain, Nellie finally reaches him. Surrounded by his jeering and taunting pals, he laughs at his sister's foolish begging. Nellie weeps at his harshness. She tells him of his mother's broken heart. She gives him a letter of love, written in his father's hand. The scenes of home wash young Willie's mind and the disease of wantonness sickens him. Before long, says Papa, Willie is led back home by his little sister.

The children enjoy Papa's nice story, as always. But there are two footnotes we need to know. First, the story Papa tells his children that night is actually the story of his own life. His name is Willie, and it was his own dear sister Nellie who, one day, years before, came looking for him in the shadowed dens of Edinburgh. Second, George MacDonald gives the tale a subtitle. He calls it "A Scot's Christmas Story." So it is, for the story of Jesus is not first of all a bland tale of pious peace or a study in theological ethics. Rather, it is a rescue story always told best in the first person. Jesus, the Good Shepherd, came from home looking through the streets and alleys of earth's slums for *me*! For *you*!

Acts 2:42-47

Margaret Mead said the first sign of civilization was found where archaeologists uncovered human skeletons with broken femur bones that had healed. The law of the jungle is, "If you fall, you die." Anyone who broke a femur had fallen and could not get away. If a skeleton displayed a healed femur it meant that someone stood between this crippled person and the danger that threatened, took this person to a place of safety, and cared for this person during a time of healing, bringing food and water, and providing protection. A healed femur, said Mead, was the telltale sign of a community that had learned to value life, care for others, and build a network of supportive relationships.

That powerful image could well be the visualization of this passage. The first evidence of Jesus' resurrection power shaping a community of the future kingdom of God is seen here at the close of Peter's Pentecost sermon. It is a strong church that breathes with God's redemptive life in Jesus. It honors the diversity of God's family, expresses optimistic faith, draws others with magnetic love, and celebrates the great king and his kingdom.

Seven themes emerge from Luke's terse description. First, this was a community of humility, living under the authority of the apostles and the guidance of their teaching. Second, this was a community of mutual care, building relationships that were deeper than a puddle after an overnight rain. Third, this was a community that rooted itself in the rituals of Jesus, remembering through sacramental rites the essentials of redemptive history. Fourth, this was a community of spiritual passion, wrestling with God in prayer for themselves and their neighbors and world. Fifth, this was a community of generosity, giving and sharing and ensuring that the poor were constantly resourced. Sixth, this was a community of worship, which amounted to a public declaration of loyalty to God and allegiance to a particular interpretation of the divine cause. Seventh, this was a missionary community, seeking constantly to bring neighbors and coworkers into the fellowship through evangelistic outreach.

Whether Luke's description of the early church is merely factual reporting or somewhat idealized in its expression, the qualities he notes are those that Jesus and the apostles constantly hold up as virtuous. Most congregations need to be reminded of these spiritual characteristics over and over again. Sometimes, however, in times of revival or unusual stress, they seem to leap to the surface.

In his book *To End All Wars* (Zondervan, 2002), Ernest Gordon tells of what he and others experienced in the Japanese prisoner-of-war camp made famous by the movie *The Bridge over the River Kwai*. The camp stood at the end of the Bataan death march that brought Allied soldiers deep into the jungles of Asia. Few would survive and everyone knew it. In order to make the best of a terrible situation they teamed up in pairs, each watching out for a buddy. One prisoner was a strapping six-foot-three fellow built like a tower of iron, but his buddy got malaria. The smaller fellow was much weaker and very likely to die. Their captors did not want to deal with sickness, so anyone who was unable to work was confined in a "hot house" until he succumbed to heat exhaustion, dehydration, and the collapse of his bodily systems. The sick man was locked in a hothouse and left to die. Surprisingly he did not die, because every mealtime his strong buddy went out to him, under curses and threats from the guards, and shared his meager rations. Every night his buddy braved the watchful eyes above that held guns of death and brought his own slim blanket to cover the fevered convulsions of the sick man.

At the end of two weeks the sick man astounded the guards by recovering well enough to be able to return to work. He even survived the entire camp experience and lived to tell about it. His buddy, however — the strong man all thought invincible — died very shortly of malaria, exposure, and dysentery. He had given his life to save his friend. The story does not end there. When Allied troops liberated that camp at the close of the war in the Pacific, virtually every prisoner was a Christian. There was a symphony orchestra in camp, with instruments made of the crudest materials. There were worship services every Sunday, and the death toll was far lower than any expected. All this because of the silent testimony made by a strong man toward his buddy facing death, and the realization that apart from Jesus' forgiving grace that develops God's new humanity, we devolve into mere animals. We need a divine shepherd to create community and guide us home.

1 Peter 2:19-25

Peter's letter appears to be a teaching handbook primarily addressed to those recently baptized into the Christian church. Persecution faced these new believers and suffering is a constant theme of the letter (see 1:6-7; 3:14-17; 4:1; 4:12-19; 5:1; 5:8-10). Here Peter calls for moral strength through suffering, patterned after Jesus' own response to his walk of pain toward the cross. The theme verse that jumps out as a badge to be worn by believers is verse 21. It was used effectively by Charles Sheldon to shape his classic Christian novel *In His Steps*, where a town is transformed by people who begin to ask themselves, "What would Jesus do?" (The WWJD bracelets made popular a decade or so ago emerged from a second "revival" of this creed.)

Peter points to Jesus as the shepherd who leads through trial and offers an example for others who struggle with life. One story from our recent history comes to mind. A young woman stared in disbelief as the Queen of England, Elizabeth II, approached her in open sight of thousands of people and hundreds of television cameras, and crowned her tennis champion of the world. It was the culmination of a powerful story of perseverance, since young Althea Gibson was born in poverty and suffered crushing childhood illnesses that left her muscles weak and her limbs twisted. It was the perseverance of Althea's mother that made the difference. Mrs. Gibson one day pointed to a rock across the yard that looked like an overgrown potato. "I want you to go down there and bring it up to the house," said her mother, "so we can use it as a step by the kitchen door."

The girl sobbed and protested. "Mommy!" she lamented, "I'm so weak that I can hardly even walk down there! How can I possibly move a stone that big?"

Her mother persisted and simply said, "You can do it! I have confidence in you! You'll figure something out."

Indeed, inch by inch, rolling and tugging and pushing, the young lass moved that rock to the house. It took her two months to do what a healthy child would have accomplished in fifteen minutes but as she tussled with the stone, Althea's muscles strengthened and her limbs straightened. Surprised by her new energy, she began a rigorous training program that led to tennis and ultimately to Wimbledon. It was there that Althea Gibson was crowned victor by the Queen of England before an awestruck world.

In Althea's view the story revolved not around her own ability to see things through but rather focused on her mother's steadfast presence. Perseverance was, for her, not so much the confidence of winning at Wimbledon or inventing something new or succeeding in business. Rather, it was being able to count on a relationship that would never let her down, even if she did not accomplish great things.

That is what Peter has in mind as well when he writes about developing perseverance in faith. Perhaps we will be fortunate enough to celebrate our dreams come true. Yet whether we win or lose in life, faith's perseverance reminds us that Jesus our shepherd will always be there for us. That is reward enough for both time and eternity.

John 10:1-10

While this passage stops just short of Jesus' multiple declarations, "I am the good shepherd" (vv. 11, 14), it breathes with the essence of that testimony (see vv. 2-4). Coming between stories of spiritual blindness (ch. 9) and antagonistic unbelief (10:22-39), Jesus' words about thieves, robbers, and strangers who lead Jesus' sheep to destruction are very pointed. They may even have caused some of the backlash in 10:22-39 (see vv. 26-27).

Though the sheep pen (v. 1) where the sheep belong may refer to many things (general well-being, the church community, eternal life, and the like), there is good reason to view it primarily as the realm of the dead. Bad shepherds, thieves, and strangers seek to bring the sheep into a twilight world of pain and judgment at death, but Jesus brings his sheep into the eternal kingdom of life (v. 10). Confirmation for this interpretation comes from the story of the raising of Lazarus in chapter 11. Lazarus has been stolen away by death, but Jesus stands in the cemetery and *calls his name* (11:43), and from the sheep pen of the great thief, Lazarus hears his name and comes out to follow his true shepherd!

Among the representations of Jesus found carved above the burial niches in the catacombs of Rome are pictures of Jesus as Orpheus. The legend of Orpheus told of his journey into the underworld to reclaim his loved Eurydice. While early Christians did not believe in the myths of Rome and Greece, they did see in this story a meaningful way to summarize the truths of John 10 — Jesus alone is the Good Shepherd who can go into the underworld where the thief has stolen away Jesus' sheep; Jesus alone has the power to challenge the thief, call his sheep by name, bring them back to life, and lead them into eternal pastures of grace, mercy, and peace.

Application

In Christopher Fry's play, *The Lady's Not for Burning*, Margaret and Nicholas are talking about a woman who seems to be acting strangely. Margaret says, "She must be lost."

Nicholas responds, wistfully, "Who isn't? The best thing we can do is to make whatever we're lost in look as much like home as we can."

That is what we do with our lives, isn't it? We have so many goals and dreams and hopes in life, yet so few of them turn out. We get old before we have done half of what we wanted. Somehow we never become what we thought we might. We make a few mistakes along the way. We disappoint some people, and they disappoint us. Even our best times have an edge of bitterness attached to them — when they end we walk away nursing our nostalgia. We are always a little bit away from home — from the home we remember or the home we desire, from the dream we miss or the dream we are still looking for. That is what Nicholas is saying to Margaret in Christopher Fry's play. We are all a bit lost in life. We are all a bit away from home. The best we can do is make what we have look as much as possible like what we think "home" should be, until we can finally see our true home and like James says, bring our friends along with us.

No matter where we go, no matter what we do, there must live in each of us a touch of that homesickness, or we die a horrible death. Our trips "home" are only a pale imitation of the place we belong and merely a wayside rest stop on a restless journey to the real home of God's love and God's eternity. More than we know, that is where we all truly want to go and only in finding Jesus and the coming of God's kingdom will our desires find fulfillment and our longings be satisfied. Only then will our homesickness end.

This is what Acts 2:42-47 pictures. This is the pilgrimage to which Peter calls us. This is the assurance that Jesus communicates when he stands and speaks as our shepherd. In him alone we find safety, even as we respond to his call into the wilds.

An Alternative Application

The picture of the church in Acts 2:24-27 is such a powerful picture that it makes a great stand-alone text for a message. In addition to the seven characteristics noted above, this passage can be used to reflect on how we can be and become more faithful in the expressions of these qualities.

One of my favorite parables related to this picture of the church is one in which the abbot of a dying monastery and a local Jewish rabbi meet regularly in the woods to commune and commiserate. Both are discouraged with the lack of faith and practice in their worlds. The elderly abbot complains about the crusty feistiness of the remaining four monks under his care — all old, all crotchety, all difficult. On one of these meetings the Jewish rabbi brings a prophetic message that he himself is mystified by. He tells the abbot that he doesn't know why, but he feels compelled to inform his friend that one among those at the monastery is the Messiah. Both feel embarrassed by this obviously inappropriate declaration and soon part to return to their homes.

At supper that evening, the abbot hesitantly tells of the rabbi's strange message. All five men laugh self-consciously and quickly move on to other conversation. But in the days that follow, the atmosphere in the monastery begins to change. Could Brother John be the Messiah? Does Brother Elred speak with divine wisdom? Is the tenacious care that the abbot gives a reflection of his holy office?

Within a month the quality of life in the monastery has changed. Those who live in the neighborhood notice it and begin attending worship services in the monastery chapel. Families enjoy picnics on the lawns of the monastery, just to be near the older men who are wiser and kinder than any seemed to remember. Then several young men asked to take vows to join the monastery, and before long, the monastery became the thriving center of a new city. They no longer call it a monastery. Instead, they have posted signs at every entrance, welcoming all to come and join "Christ's Community." Indeed, Messiah is among them!

Between acts

What do you do between Act 2 and Act 3 of a performance? That depends upon who you are.

If you are like me, then you have attended a great many more shows, plays, and performances than you have participated in. As members of the audience, the time between acts is an intermission — an opportunity to stretch your legs, to use the restroom, to enjoy some refreshments.

If you have ever been part of the stage crew for some performance, however, then you understand the minutes between acts quite differently. It is not a casual and relaxing time. On the contrary, it is a period marked by hustle and hard work. There's a clear sense of what needs to be done — moved, changed, turned, or whatever else — in order to be prepared for the next act, and the stage crew member who decides that intermission would be a good time to use the restroom and get a drink will not keep his job for long.

As followers of Christ, we are not invited to be mere spectators. We find ourselves living in the meantime — in the minutes between God's great acts — and one of these days, we know that the curtain will suddenly go up, and the star of the show will make his grand entrance for the final act. Our job is not to stretch our legs, get a cold drink, and wait it out. Our job is to make sure that the stage is set and everything is prepared for what and who is to come.

Acts 7:55-60

This scene opens with a reference to the Holy Spirit.

At a human level, that is of course characteristic of the author, Luke. He is more attentive to the Holy Spirit as a theme than any of the other gospel writers (compare, for example, Matthew 7:11 and Luke 11:13), and Luke uses the phrase "filled with the Holy Spirit" ten times in his gospel and in Acts.

Meanwhile, at a spiritual level, the phenomenon doesn't trace back to Luke; he is just the one most deliberately reporting it. Rather, there is this presence and activity of the Holy Spirit and that is especially central to the story of Acts. Indeed, many have suggested that the book might be more appropriately titled "The Acts of the Holy Sprit" than "The Acts of the Apostles."

See the snapshot of this particular scene in your mind's eye. Freeze the picture and zoom in to get a closer look at the faces. Where do you see peace and where do you see agitation? Where do you see hands raised up in a kind of desperate self-defense and where do you see a placid strength?

On the one hand, you have a crowd with fistfuls of stones. On the other hand, you have an innocent victim, harassed, defenseless, and facing a gruesome execution. Yet it is the crowd that is agitated. They are the ones raising their hands to cover their ears. Stephen, by contrast, seems very much at peace. He makes no apparent effort to resist them or to defend himself. His effort is only to bear witness to Christ and to pray for his tormentors' forgiveness. Stephen puts flesh and blood on that magnificent line from Charles Wesley's hymn: "Happy, if with my latest breath I may but gasp his name, preach him to all and cry in death, 'Behold, behold the Lamb!'" (Charles Wesley, "Jesus! The Name High Over All").

We know the look of the child who, in a tantrum, refuses to listen. He covers his ears, stamps his feet, and wails, "I'm not listening to you!" or "I can't hear you!" That is the look of Stephen's persecutors. They find his words intolerable, unbearable, and so they cover their ears, shout loudly, and hurry to shut him up. But the word of God cannot be shut up (see Jeremiah 20:9; 2 Timothy 2:9). It cannot be contained within an individual. Then much to the consternation of its opponents, even after that individual is silenced, the word of God still cannot be contained.

The great dramatic irony of the scene, of course, is the figure of the young man with the coats draped at his feet. Little did that indignant and bloodthirsty mob know that, while they rushed to silence one voice for Christ, perhaps the man who would become his greatest evangelist was standing there in their midst. He observed, approved, and emulated their zealous persecution. Within a few years, however, that same man would be spanning the Mediterranean proclaiming the same Jesus whose name and whose message that crowd found intolerable.

For preaching purposes, this passage can be taken in several directions. First, there is the theme of the Holy Spirit's activity — within history, within the early church, and within an individual's life — that could be explored in light of Stephen's story and example. Second, there is the character Stephen himself: initially designated to do a seemingly less important work (Acts 6:1-5), and yet in the end, a tremendous witness and example, the first Christian martyr, and the person who has the longest recorded sermon in the book of Acts. Third, there is the response of the crowd: Why does the affirmation of Christ at the right hand of God, both then and now, evoke such violent opposition? Fourth, there is the story of Saul, pondering what long-term influence this episode may have had on him (see, for example, 2 Timothy 4:16).

1 Peter 2:2-10

Mother's milk. It is, I suppose, the most natural thing in the world. As my wife and I read and learned about breastfeeding when our children were born, we were continually amazed by the beauty of the whole design. How this brand new baby, who didn't know anything, knew what to do when she was put on her mother's breast. How everything that she needed — and would need for some months — was contained in that simple, natural formula. How nutrition, comfort, and relationship all came together in a single act. Beautiful.

Meanwhile, our ten-year-old daughter was at an extended family event recently and one of her aunts offered her a taste of coffee. The aunt is a real coffee lover — even a bit of a coffee snob — and so she was sharing with our daughter one of her great pleasures in life. When our daughter tasted it, however, she did not see the appeal. Her aunt read her reaction on her face and replied, "It's an acquired taste."

So it is that the newborn is so naturally drawn to its mother's perfect milk. And so it is that, as we age, we acquire so many other tastes — some of them quite unhealthy for us.

One wonders what Peter's congregation had acquired tastes for. What imperfect, impure, ultimately undesirable things they desired and consumed. Whatever they were, Peter wanted to see them return to what's best — a spiritual version of the pure and perfect mother's milk.

We, and our congregations, would be well served to consider the same question. What unhealthy tastes have we acquired? What do we consume that is so far removed from the pure spiritual milk God has for us?

Next, that exhortation to desire spiritual milk leads Peter into an inspired and poetic invitation to the Lord himself. Here is where the passage becomes a theological statement about the person and work of Christ.

The primary imagery of the passage is stones. If you have a teaching or expository style of preaching, then this Sunday's sermon may be found in the development of that one theme. We'll look more carefully at some of the options involved here below.

In the end, Peter references four different Old Testament texts in this brief passage. Verse 6 quotes from Isaiah 28:16. Verse 7 comes from Psalm 118:22. Verse 8 cites Isaiah 8:14 and verse 10 recalls Hosea 1:9-10. All of this is in addition to verse 9, which is full of images that find elaboration and meaning in

Old Testament texts about Israel and Levi.

This tapestry of Old Testament references — whether by direct quote or by borrowed imagery — reminds us of several realities within the early church and its preaching.

First, its text, its scripture, was the Old Testament, not the New. In the modern American church, the Old Testament is so often dismissed as outdated, irrelevant, even replaced. We do well to remember that the apostles managed to preach the gospel from the law, the prophets, and the writings.

Second, the early church understood itself and Jesus in light of the Old Testament. Where we get our understanding of "church" has a tremendous influence on where our churches struggle and what our churches become. Do we operate out of a paradigm of what we're used to or what we grew up with? Do we borrow our understanding from the business world or from a marketing and advertising age? The early church understood itself in light of Old Testament paradigms — holy priesthood, spiritual sacrifices, chosen race, royal priesthood, holy nation, and such. Our congregations may need to be reacquainted with those truths.

Third, the early church employed a hermeneutic that was perfectly willing to excerpt a single verse here and there in order to illustrate a point. This should not, I think, be confused with proof-texting. They were under no pressure — particularly in the latter first-century as the church's chief opponent became not the Jews but the pagan Romans — to manipulate scripture to their purposes. Rather, they readily welcomed as being from God any text or phrase from scripture that seemed to be given new and fuller meaning by Christ.

John 14:1-14

Here is a favorite passage of scripture for so many people. Or, perhaps more accurately, here in this one passage are found three different favorite passages — favorites for different people and for different occasions.

First, here is a favorite passage for funeral services. After Psalm 23, I suppose the early verses of John 14 are the ones I have most often had grieving family members request to have read at their loved one's funeral. We cherish the image of Jesus preparing a place for us and the promise that he will "come again and take (us) to (himself)."

Second, here is a favorite passage for evangelism and for discussions of Christology. For starters, there is another of the "I am" statements of Jesus that are so central to the gospel of John: "I am the way, the truth, and the life." Follow several significant claims of Christ about his identity with the Father: no one comes to the Father but through him, whoever has seen him has seen the Father, and he is in the Father and the Father is in him.

Finally, here is a favorite passage for prayer. Jesus boldly promises that "I will do whatever you ask in my name" and "if in my name you ask me for anything, I will do it." To the skeptical observer, it seems like a reckless kind of statement. To the earnest petitioner, however, it is the very fuel of faith.

Charles Spurgeon, the great nineteenth-century preacher, offers helpful insight into this seemingly blank check signed by Jesus. "Does the text mean what it says? I never knew my Lord to say anything he did not mean... mind you, he does not say to all men, 'I will give you whatever you ask.' That would be an unkind kindness. But he speaks to his disciples who have already received great grace at his hands. It is to disciples he commits this marvelous power of prayer" (Charles Spurgeon, *The Power of Prayer in a Believer's Life* [Lynnwood, Washington: Emerald Books, 1993], p. 35).

In the end, of course, there is something very right about this combination of favorite Bible verses. It is right that these things should be all woven together: who Jesus is in relation to the Father, in relation to us, what we can do for him, what he can do through us, and all that he and the Father have in store. While the familiar verses in this passage may be siphoned off individually for their own use and meaning, they are best understood all together, for they are part of a natural whole. We cannot properly separate our Christology from our hope of heaven, on the one hand, nor from our faith on earth, on the other.

Application

Our lections for this week prompt us to think about life in the meantime: life lived in service to Christ between acts.

In John, we see him on the verge of his exit. He tells his followers that he is about to go and that he is going to come back, and thanks to Stephen's vision in the book of Acts, meanwhile, we catch a brief glimpse of where he has gone: "I see the heavens opened and the Son of Man standing at the right hand of God!" Stephen's testimony brings to mind the familiar words of the Apostles' Creed — he "sitteth at the right hand of God the Father Almighty" — and what follows — "from thence he shall come to judge the quick and the dead."

Bob Kauflin sets the two acts side by side in his song, "In The First Light." View the lyrics at www.cybertime.net/~ajgood/firstlight.html.

We live between those acts, preparing and setting the stage for his return. We see that we are empowered and encouraged in that work by Jesus himself: "The one who believes in me will also do the works that I do and, in fact, will do greater works than these, because I am going to the Father."

We also see in Peter's epistle something of our job description. Words like "royal," "priesthood," "holy," and "chosen" signify the purposeful and differentiated existence to which we are called. These are not the terms that belong to spectators in the lobby. These make up the calling of people with serious and urgent work to do.

We see in Stephen the look of that service. Here is where the stage crew metaphor breaks down, for the analogy only speaks to our timing and purpose, not to our experience. For as long as we are in this world, we are opposed. This stage violently resists being set.

Yet, in the face of all that, we also see our reward. Stephen saw it and we sense it in his face and in his words. Jesus promised it to his disciples: the stage that he himself is setting and the preparation that he is making for us! Such a way for the star to spend this intermission!

An Alternative Application

1 Peter 2:2-10. We noted above that this passage from 1 Peter makes much use of the image of stones. In fact, it becomes an extended metaphor, and we might explore the depth of what Peter is saying by identifying the different relationships to "the stone" that Peter suggests here. That stone represents Jesus and that is a relationship worth considering.

First, there is God's relationship to the stone. It is precious to him, established by him, and central to his work and purpose in the world.

Second, there is the relationship to the stone of those who oppose it. They try to reject it, though they find futility in fighting God's own purpose. (The persecutors of Stephen are a good example of that useless opposition.) And more than rejecting it, it becomes "a stone that makes them stumble, and a rock that makes them fall."

In his 1985 album, *Scandalon*, Michael Card provocatively considers this text, as well as our contemporary situation: Check out the lyrics at www.lyricz.net/C/Card+Michael/89098/.

Third, there is the relationship to the stone of those who "come to him." To us, as to God, he is precious. By coming to him, we ourselves are "built into a spiritual house," and so, in direct contrast to those who futilely oppose what God is doing, it is our privilege to be incorporated into what God is doing.

Finally, in addition to the multi-level references to stones and rocks within the confines of this passage, there are several other points that you may want to employ, whether in the sermon, the hymns, or the scripture readings and liturgy.

First, there is the long-standing tradition of identifying God with a rock (see, for example, Psalm 18:2, 46; 31:3; 61:2; 62:2). It is an image that conveys strength, stability, and protection.

Second, there is the irony that, in the Acts passage, stones become the weapon of choice in trying to silence Stephen. Thus, on the one hand, you have the stone chosen by God and made the cornerstone. On the other hand, you have the small and destructive stones chosen by the antagonists. One is established with purpose, while the others are flung in anger. One is built upon, while the others are scattered. One endures, while the others are dust.

Third, there is the personal component involved in all of this imagery for Peter. Here is the one who grew up as "Simon," but who was renamed by his Lord "Peter," which means "rock." One cannot ignore how central and significant the imagery Peter employs here must have been to him personally.

Our known God

Pulling off the exit ramp on a highway in Pennsylvania, I saw a sign that caught my attention. It was part of a collection of blue informational signs that featured no words, just icons accompanied by directional arrows. For example, here was a little blue sign with images of a fork and spoon on it, along with an arrow pointing to the left. Then there was a sign with a little gas pump icon and another arrow pointing to the left. Next there was a sign with a picture of a tent and an arrow pointing to the right. Finally, there was a sign with a question mark on it, and an arrow pointing to the right.

Now I presume that the question mark was the icon for some sort of an information center or travel center. Still, when I first saw it, it amused me. It was as if these signs were saying, "We know that food is over here, and so is fuel. We know that if you want to camp, you can just turn this way. And then, farther down that road... well, we're not quite sure what it is... but we know it's that way!"

That is exactly the kind of sign that the apostle Paul saw in the ancient city of Athens. The people there had a vague belief in an "unknown god." They had an altar erected in his honor. But he remained a question mark to the ancient Athenians.

That god was not unknown to Paul, however. And he is not unknown to us.

As we consider the apostle's visit to Athens, along with the counsel of Peter and the promises of Christ in this week's lections, we will affirm that our God is, indeed, known — known and knowable. So we go off into our world with the same calling and opportunity as Paul: to make known the Lord among people who do not know him yet.

Acts 17:22-31

We are fortunate to have a record of Paul's visit to Athens and especially his presentation before the Areopagus. In this brief passage, Paul conducts a veritable clinic on evangelism. It is a model of what to do, as well as a concrete reminder of what not to do.

What Paul does not do is take the ever-winsome holier-than-thou approach. He certainly believes that his audience is intellectually misguided and spiritually lost, but that is not the message he gives them or the tone with which he addresses them. He could have told them that they were misguided and lost, and he would have been right. But being right is not the only ingredient in evangelism.

Neither does he take a smarter-than-thou approach. His message was arguably that they did not really know what to believe, and so he was there to tell them what to believe. But that was not the attitude of his presentation. One senses that Paul was side-by-side with them, rather than talking down to them, even as he endeavored to lead them to the truth.

Meanwhile, we should note that Paul also does not take the live-and-let-live approach. This is the posture that is most at home in the pluralism of our own culture, but it was not Paul's *modus operandi*. He did not say to himself, "These people clearly already have their own beliefs, their own religions, and they're very earnest about it all. I should not force my beliefs on them." That mentality would have seemed nonsensical to Paul.

Too often, in some circles, Christians navigate by the stars of purity and orthodoxy, and in the process they judge and condemn people for where they are. In other circles, Christians will too often set their compass toward tolerance, and thus leave people where they are deliberately undisturbed. Paul, by contrast, met the Athenians where they were and he endeavored to lead them where they needed to be.

In Athens, Paul encountered a population that was religious and educated and he worked with that. "I see how extremely religious you are in every way," he remarks to his audience. It is winsome and complimentary. He might have looked at precisely the same evidence and said, "I see how extremely pagan and confused you are in every way," but that would not have earned the gospel much of a hearing. And so he used their religiousness — indeed, even their idolatry — to his advantage.

Paul also demonstrated his meet-them-where-they're-at approach in the material that he did and did not quote. "As even some of your own poets have said," Paul preached, "we too are his offspring." Now Paul would not have regarded ancient Greek poets as highly as he did the canon of Hebrew scripture. But quoting the Hebrew scriptures would not have scored any points — would not even have made a connection — with his audience. And so, even though the one source had infinitely more value for Paul, he chose to cite the source that would have had more value for his audience.

Finally, we see that Paul also encountered in Athens a people who clearly had some uncertainty — or at least some questions and openness. He made that his welcome mat. "What therefore you worship as unknown," Paul said, "this I proclaim to you." He does not march into town, knock over all of their existing beliefs, and try to erect his own in their place. No, he takes what they already believe and he builds on it. "I've come to tell you about the 'unknown god,'" Paul said in effect, "because I know him."

1 Peter 3:13-22

Unjust suffering is no small theme in scripture. We see it almost from the beginning, in the murder of the innocent Abel. Young Joseph, whose story is one of the longest narratives about any individual character in the entire Old Testament, chronicles the unjust treatment of an innocent man — as well as the prevailing providence of God. We think, too, of David — faultlessly loyal to King Saul, yet hunted and hounded by the madman king through the deserts and caves of the Judean wilderness. Job, Jeremiah, and a number of anonymous psalmists are all part of this large contingent of suffering saints, "of whom the world was not worthy" (Hebrews 11:38).

But there is one more, and he is in a class by himself. The ultimate instance of unjust suffering is Jesus Christ. His case is unique, for he was more innocent than all the rest, and his suffering was also at a different level than the rest.

The people in Peter's audience were evidently suffering. In ten verses, he makes five references to "suffer" or "suffering." It was a theme relevant to those Christians, whom he regarded as exiles (1:1) — that is, alien residents; men and women, whose real home is elsewhere and who live for the present in hostile territory. As he wrote to them in the midst of their struggles, Jesus was very much on Peter's mind.

Perhaps Peter had Jesus' teachings in mind as he wrote. "If you do suffer for doing right," Peter said, "you are blessed." It may be that the aging apostle remembered that lovely day by Galilee, hearing his master and teacher say something which, at the time, seemed completely irrational to him: "Blessed are those who are persecuted for righteousness' sake, for theirs is the kingdom of heaven. Blessed are you when people revile you and persecute you and utter all kinds of evil against you falsely on my account. Rejoice and be glad, for your reward is great in heaven, for in the same way they persecuted the prophets who were before you" (Matthew 5:10-12).

I imagine that Peter had Jesus' example in mind, as well. He encouraged his congregations that "those who abuse you for your good conduct in Christ may be put to shame." Peter had seen that at work. He had watched the conspiring mob drop their stones and walk away (see John 8:2-9). And he had seen those who tried to lay traps befuddled and frustrated (see Matthew 22:15-46).

No doubt, Peter also had a certain personal lesson from Jesus in mind. The first he had heard of Christ's sufferings, Peter had objected that it should never happen (Mark 8:31-33). Now, on the other side of the cross and the empty tomb, Peter had grown out of his natural human instinct about such matters and he writes with understanding, "It is better to suffer for doing good, if suffering should be God's will."

Then, with all of that in mind, Peter begins to think about Jesus' saving work. The concern for his audience's suffering had moved him to consider Christ's suffering. That, in turn, led him to the greatest encouragements of all: about Christ bringing us to God, our salvation, and the ultimate victory, glory, and authority of Jesus Christ.

John 14:15-21

Love is an important theme in the Johannine literature in the New Testament. It is John's gospel that features the great statement of God's motivation and purpose — "for God so loved the world" — that some have called it "the gospel in a nutshell." It is John's gospel that features the new love commandment (13:34), as well as identifying love as the ultimate proof of whom we follow (13:35). In 1 John, we are introduced to the inarguable logic of love (4:19-21), and we are taught that love is the essential attribute of God (4:8). Even in John's Revelation, amidst spectacles of glory and terror, amidst the cataclysms of the eschaton, there is a poignant appeal to lost love (2:4-5).

In light of that larger theme, then, we are interested to note this truth about love: that it leads to obedience.

This is a point of enormous theological importance, for it gives insight into why God did what he did from the beginning. For we recognize that God could have created us in such a way that we would have obeyed by design. That suggests a human creature, however, that is not free, and therefore one that could not genuinely love. So, instead, God preferred to make a creature capable of love, though consequently free, and therefore susceptible to disobedience.

But this was God's wisdom, for the relationship between love and obedience is not a two-way street. Obedience will not necessarily lead to love. All sorts of joyless and judgmental legalists through the ages bear witness to that. But Jesus says that love, on the other hand, will lead to obedience.

Another significant theme of this passage is the Trinity. There may be no passage in scripture more revealing about the Trinity than these Last Supper chapters in John. Here Jesus speaks repeatedly and freely about his relationship to the Father and to the Spirit.

In our brief excerpt from that larger context, Jesus refers to the Spirit as "another Advocate." Interestingly, John uses that same word for Jesus in his own first epistle (1 John 2:1). Perhaps that explains Jesus using the term "another." In any case, the word is used only five times in the entire New Testament. Four of them are here in this section of John's gospel and the other is the reference to Jesus in the epistle.

Outside of the New Testament, the underlying Greek word was often used in a legal context. And it had a natural counterpart, an opposite: accuser. That is noteworthy for us since, in the King James Version, Satan is referred to as "the accuser of our brethren... which accused them before our God day and night" (Revelation 12:10 KJV). We see that it is Satan who points the finger of accusation against us, while the Spirit and Son of God speak on our behalf.

Finally, in addition to Jesus' frequent references to himself, the Father, and the Spirit in relation to one another, this passage — and its larger context — also offers another significant insight into the Trinity. Again and again, the followers of Jesus are brought into the mix. The persons of the Trinity are not a clique, separate and self-contained. Rather, we ourselves are invited into that divine fellowship. So Jesus explains to his disciples that the Spirit "abides in you." Later, he says, "I am in my Father, and you in me, and I in you." The Trinity may be a mystery to us but this much we may understand: It is a unity and fellowship of love and we are invited into it.

Application

When I was traveling down that one highway, I came across a blue informational sign with a question mark and an arrow pointing off to the right.

When the apostle Paul was traveling in ancient Athens, he came across an altar dedicated to an unknown God.

What Paul saw was a theological version of the sign that I had seen along the highway. Here was an altar with a question mark on it and an arrow pointing up. We don't know what it is but we know it's up there. We don't know who he is but we know he's out there. We don't know what he's like but we've got an altar here where we can worship him.

We, too, live in a time and place of spiritual uncertainty. The people around us have question marks all over their altars. That is to say, uncertainty pervades their sense of meaning and purpose, their understanding of the world, and their assumptions about the spiritual and the supernatural. There is no lack of interest but there is a profound lack of personal knowledge and familiarity.

We also live in the midst of a relativism that betrays the prevailing uncertainty. The mere fact that our culture is so ready to accept every belief, practice, and paradigm as equally valid bears witness to our lack of conviction. Our relativism is simply codified uncertainty.

Sports pundits like to say of teams with quarterback controversies, "If you think you have two starting quarterbacks, then you don't really have any starting quarterback." Likewise, if we think we have a hundred truths, we don't really have any truths.

So it may be that contemporary America is not so different from ancient Athens. Our God is unknown here too. Not that he is unheard of, as Jesus mostly was in first-century Greece. But he is unknown. He is vague impressions and misinformation. He is locked back in the mists of history. He is a question mark.

Jesus told his disciples that "the world cannot receive" the Spirit of truth "because it neither sees him nor knows him." He is, indeed, unknown to the world around us. But he is not unknown to us. "You know him," Jesus said, "because he abides with you, and he will be in you."

Like Paul, we travel among people with question marks on their altars. Our calling is to proclaim the one who is unknown to them, for we know him. We affirm that he is knowable. For this is, after all, the God who came to meet us where we are; who put on flesh and dwelt among us; who said, "Whoever has seen me has seen the Father" (John 14:9).

Our altars do not have a question mark with an arrow pointing vaguely upward. Rather, our altars have an exclamation point with an arrow directing the world's attention to Jesus Christ.

An Alternative Application

Acts 17:22-31. "Altar avenue." The apostle Paul was a big-city missionary. By the end of his journeys, he had taken the gospel to all the major cities in the first-century Mediterranean world, from Jerusalem to Rome, Antioch and Ephesus, Philippi, Thessalonica, Corinth, and more.

One of the characteristics of big cities, of course, is that certain types of businesses tend to congregate together along a single road or in a particular location. So, for example, here's a strip where four or five different car dealerships have all set up shop. Here's an intersection where five different motel chains are all located. Here's a shopping mall whose parking lot is rimmed by every imaginable family restaurant. And so on.

The most famous instances of this happens to be in New York City. One particular street, where several major advertising firms located years ago, has become synonymous with that industry: Madison Avenue. Likewise, the concentration of financial institutions on a single street have made the name of that street — Wall Street — mean business and finance. And the strip of theaters along a single road has made the name of that road the embodiment of the theater: Broadway.

Perhaps the ancient, big city of Athens had such a street: a particular part of town where all the shrines, idols, and temples were built. Call it "Altar Avenue." When the apostle Paul comes to town, he walks that wide way and shakes his head at the idolatry and confusion all around him.

We observed, in our discussion of the Acts passage, how exemplary was Paul's presentation of the gospel in Athens. We should learn from him, for we walk down our own "Altar Avenues" in our day. Indeed, I would make the claim that we not only have more people than the ancient city of Athens; we also have more altars.

By "altar" I do not exclusively mean a designated sacred spot where offerings are presented. Ultimately an altar is not defined by its look, design, or dimensions. Rather, an altar is defined by what takes place there.

We might invite our people — and ourselves — to ponder for a few moments what it is that takes place at an altar.

Wherever you see individuals dedicating themselves, where they serve with all their allegiance, where they affirm their top priority, their guiding principles, and their mission, where they find their sense of meaning and purpose in life — those settings serve as altars, and we have scores of people around us who wander from altar to altar, filled with question marks.

If we would learn from the apostle, we would recognize the altars in our world for what they are. We would meet people there and redirect their attention to the one who is truly worthy of that devotion and role in their hearts and lives.

Ascension of Our Lord
Acts 1:1-11
Ephesians 1:15-23
Luke 24:44-53
by R. Craig MacCreary

Ground rules

This past summer I was treated to viewing one of those baseball donnybrooks in which managers and players are freely tossed out of the game. It came on a play that you would not think should be the cause of such consternation: a home run over the centerfield wall. It seems things were a bit complicated in this minor league park. In order for it to be a home run, the ball had to clear a yellow line where the flat level of an outdoor restaurant met the wall of the ballpark. This was all made a lot more difficult by the fact that one umpire called it a home run only to have the head umpire call it all back. It also struck me as interesting that the dispute broke out even though the umpires and managers met at the beginning to go over the ground rules of the game and of the grounds of this particular park. The game only went on after several ejections and it was evident to all concerned that things would not proceed until all sides agreed at least that the head umpire's ruling was final, which is also one of the ground rules of the game.

As I wondered how it was that we were devoting so much time to this hiatus from the game it dawned on me how like the church was this minor league donnybrook. The rules bear repeating, things do not come back into balance until we recognize who really is in charge, and you never know when a knock-down-drag-out will occur. They will occur; they are likely to occur over something that no one has anticipated. There is nothing that can override the above facts of the game. Like life, baseball is so heavily nuanced that no one can anticipate all the possibilities ahead, knowing the rules will not prove sufficient to cover all eventualities and you will be on your own until order is restored.

In a very real sense that is how Jesus leaves his disciples following the resurrection. Even before he departs, the disciples have their questions, "So when they had come together, they asked him, 'Lord, is this the time when you will restore the kingdom to Israel?' " They have their questions but soon they will not have their Jesus to give them direct answers.

The narration of the ascension in the book of Acts focuses on the future mission of the church, while the narration in Luke focuses more on the basis of that mission as found in scripture. In both cases, Jesus is laying the groundwork for when the ground rules come into question.

Paul certainly had his share of disputes, claims, and counterclaims in the churches that he wrote and visited. The early church had its share of hardnosed moments. It is very clear that the apostles must function in the new context of having no final arbiter of their disputes. Jesus will leave them in the context of having to work out much on their own. The passage in the letter to the Ephesians, chosen as part of today's lectionary reading, seeks to identify the Jesus who is above every interpretation of the ground rules. No single interpretation can be identified with him. To do so would be like saying that one side or the other in the dispute over the home run had an exclusive franchise on the meaning of baseball. As absurd as that is, how often do various sides in church disputes go after each other, reading each other out of the Christian community?

The texts invite us to consider the ground rules by which we are playing the "game" in our disputes and conflicts. Whom do we expect to restore order? Or do we believe that we have arrived at a uniformity of understanding that will result in such conformity that it will not be necessary for there to be community guided by the Holy Spirit?

For Luke, it is essential to wait for the Holy Sprit in the life of the church. While it is the key for Luke, it often seems to be relegated to a quick prayer over meetings that include perfunctory references to the idea that we will not act until we understand that what is to be done is pleasing to both us and the Holy Spirit. While staying with them, he ordered them not to leave Jerusalem, but to wait there for the promise of the Father. "This," he said, "is what you have heard from me...."

How we understand the work of the Holy Sprit determines what we are waiting for. Do we wait for an ecstatic experience; will the sign of the Spirit's presence be the establishment of a consensus, will we understand the Spirit's presence to be manifested when everyone is happy and in their comfort zone, or when no one rests easy with things as they are? I suspect that the answer is, "Yes." Each of these expresses some of what the Spirit brings us. Paul puts it this way in the first letter to the Corinthians, "Now there are varieties of gifts, but the same Spirit; and there are varieties of services, but the same Lord; and there are varieties of activities, but it is the same God who activates all of them in everyone. To each is given the manifestation of the Spirit for the common good. To one is given through the Spirit the utterance of wisdom, and to another the utterance of knowledge according to the same Spirit, to another faith by the same Spirit, to another gifts of healing by the one Spirit, to another the working of miracles, to another prophecy, to another the discernment of spirits, to another various kinds of tongues, to another the interpretation of tongues. All these are activated by one and the same Spirit, who allots to each one individually just as the Spirit chooses" (1 Corinthians 12:4-11).

There are times when the church should be about waiting. Those occasions come in light of the absence of the physical presence as the church waits for him to be present through the gift of the Holy Spirit. How do we know that we should be waiting? I suspect that we should be waiting on the Spirit when it becomes clear in the life of a church that people are neither free nor challenged to exercise their gifts. This is a major block to the flow of the Spirit. The lesson from Acts says that the apostles are to be engaged in mission, "But you will receive power when the Holy Spirit has come upon you; and you will be my witnesses in Jerusalem, in all Judea and Samaria, and to the ends of the earth" (v. 8). It is time to wait in the Spirit if we have become disengaged from the world and our role in it. A church that is floundering in mission or is frustrating the gifts of its members has blocked the Spirit.

In the passage from Acts when the disciples have gathered, a question arises among them. So when they had come together, they asked him, "Lord, is this the time when you will restore the kingdom to Israel?" The apostles, with an understandable curiosity that is still part of the Christian experience, want to know just where they are in the unfolding plan of God. Such curiosity is often a frustration to the Spirit and a sign that folks need to wait on the fullness of time when it is appropriate for such matters to be revealed. "He replied, 'It is not for you to know the times or periods that the Father has set by his own authority.'" Needless to say there has been much theological effort thrown in to determine at just what point we are in God's unfolding intention for the world. Yet such a preoccupation is a frustration to the Spirit. A congregation so invested needs to sit down and reflect on the work of the Spirit in its midst. We are to be obedient to what God intends while not fully capable of understanding unfolding details of the plan of God.

The Acts passage warns against being transfixed by staring at the place where Jesus once was. It reminds me somewhat of any congregation that has been through a church fire. Often congregants will come for days immediately following the fire to the stare at the place where the steeple was, pondering whether the hole in the sky or in their souls will ever be filled again. The angels that appear push the apostles to move beyond staring off into the sky to the realization that Jesus will return again.

Many congregations in the mainline tradition seem to be staring off into the place where Jesus and they once were after the spiritual fire that many of them had experienced in previous years. The promise is that after the fire, Jesus will return. He may not return in the manner that we had previously experienced, as if his work was more to restore the past than lead us into the future. However, he will return with the same redemptive intention, "This Jesus, who has been taken up from you into heaven, will come in the same way as you saw him go into heaven" (v. 11). If you find yourself staring off into heaven, it is time to gather and wait on the Spirit who has more in store.

Ephesians 1:15-23

The letter reflects a close relationship between the writer and the people. "I have heard of your faith in the Lord Jesus and your love toward all the saints, and for this reason I do not cease to give thanks for you as I remember you in my prayers" (vv. 15-16). These are clearly folks with whom the letter writer has a close relationship and a deep affection. Sometimes it is very hard to pray for those with whom we are the closest. We are often afraid as they grow and develop that for one reason or the other we will lose the close relationship. A spirit of wisdom and knowledge may leave those who are closest to us in disagreement with us or ahead us of us in a way that they do not need us.

So what then should we pray for those who are particularly close to us? "I pray that the God of our Lord Jesus Christ, the Father of glory, may give you a spirit of wisdom and revelation as you come to know him" (v. 17). We do get very close to each other in church life and sometimes too close as we experience each others' foibles and are tempted to take each other for granted. Praying for each other becomes essential as the community of faith waits for the return of Jesus. It is one of the ground rules for Paul as he reminds his readers in several of his letters that he is praying for them. "I have heard of your faith in the Lord Jesus and your love toward all the saints, and for this reason I do not cease to give thanks for you as I remember you in my prayers" (vv. 15-16).

The readers of the letter to the Ephesians, by virtue of the example of the letter writer, are clearly urged to keep one another in their prayers. However, the reader is urged to offer a specific prayer. The author prays for the Ephesians that they be given a spirit of wisdom and revelation as they come to know Jesus. The prayer asks for a spirit that will give wisdom over human affairs as it anticipates the revelation of things that are hidden. Despite the nearly 2,000 years that have passed since the writing of this letter many churches find that, as they await the return of Jesus, they are in about the same place as were the Ephesians. As the "emerging church" comes into view what will be the practical consequences for "old first" mainline on the town square? How will the emerging church affect the use, renovation, or location of the church building? What will be the implications for church structure and organization? What will be the impact on those who were born into one form of church and who will now live out their days in a church context far different from the one they were born into?

Wisdom and revelation go hand in hand. One of the ground rules is to never separate the two. Without being attuned to the things that God is revealing, much of what we do in church feels like a desperate scheme to save ourselves from declining numbers and resources. On the other hand, there is nothing worse than the leader of the new wave of things who has no appreciation in human terms of what they are proposing.

When these two are held together, "... that, with the eyes of your heart enlightened, you may know what is the hope to which he has called you, what are the riches of his glorious inheritance among the saints" (v. 18). But separate the two and things are either hopelessly boring or depressingly impractical.

The Ephesians are reminded that if the spirit of wisdom and revelation are held together, they will understand the result as the work of the immeasurable power of God. The holding together of these two dimensions has carried the church up until now and will carry it into the immeasurable future until Christ returns.

Luke 24:44-53

Once again, Jesus directs his disciples to go to Jerusalem and wait until they are "clothed with power from on high" (v. 49). No doubt we are a bit uncomfortable with what appears to be a senseless repetition of the scene recounted in the book of Acts. It certainly does not meet our standard for effective writing. Of course, by this standard much of scripture does not meet the standard of effective writing. Time and again we are walked through the same territory as the stories are retold with different emphasis and through different voices.

In this context, Jesus says to the disciples, "These are my words that I spoke to you while I was still with you — that everything written about me in the law of Moses, the prophets, and the psalms must be fulfilled" (v. 44). Jesus is the extension of the witness of the Hebrew Testament. No doubt, there were times for the early church when the waters did not part and it seemed that they were so far from the promised land that it was hard to believe that they were living out God's intention, which was rooted in the Hebrew story. As they faced the interim time between the ascension and Jesus' return it must have seemed hard to believe that. I suspect as we live in the interim time it is hard to believe it when the church seems so weak and vulnerable. Part of Jesus' teaching is to remind the disciples that he, too, has gone through a time of weakness and vulnerability, "Then he opened their minds to understand the scriptures, and he said to them, 'Thus it is written, that the Messiah is to suffer and to rise from the dead on the third day' " (vv. 45-46).

The Holy Spirit is bestowed on those who must live through this time. The end product, as it were, is that the disciples can bless God even in the time of Jesus' absence. Living in this time, we must come to terms with what the Spirit promotes and pushes for as well as what it does not provide for. A sermonic illustration from my context literally as an interim pastor puts it this way, "I have known a class of people over the years that never seems to be able to settle on a church. They always seem to be searching for the perfect church where 24 hours a day, 7 days a week, everyone agrees on everything and there is perpetual conflict-free harmony. Such an approach leads to a few years here and a few years there. Always something seems to come up that sets them off church hunting once again: the church paints the bathroom the wrong color, the youth group does something wrong, or they pick the wrong minister." I suspect that these are people who are really drowning, because they have stood on what they think is the safety of the shore rather than plunging right into the waters of life. Taking the plunge means choosing to make stumbling blocks the stepping stones. If you are searching for the perfect church, you certainly would have never found it in the Bible. Just read Paul's letters. The question to be asked if looking for a church is, "Does this congregation turn its stumbling blocks (and every congregation has them) into building blocks?" Do the stumbles get turned into prayer, into more open and honest conversation, into the ability to laugh at yourself among others? The Holy Spirit will not provide a perfect church but can turn the imperfections to the glory of God and the blessing of its members. No wonder the disciples were continually in the temple praising God.

Application

It is an irony of biblical proportions that Jesus' ascension into heaven results in the establishment of some ground rules as we await his return. There are times when the church must wait on the Spirit. During the interim time, the church must hold together the spirit of wisdom and revelation, and the church must be open to what the Holy Spirit pushes and promotes as it lives with what the Spirit will not provide. I believe that this is true for all churches whatever their denominational background or history, for we are dealing here with the one who is "far above all rule and authority and power and dominion, and above every name that is named, not only in this age but also in the age to come. And he has put all things under his feet and has made him the head over all things for the church" (Ephesians 1:21-22).

I recall that the official rules of major league baseball say that the game shall commence when the umpire shall yell play. Not ball but play. I rather suspect that we lose our playfulness when we do not know or are not ready to go along with the basic ground rules.

An Alternative Application

Luke 24:44-53. One cannot read these texts without having some apocalyptic gestalt. However, much of the misery of the Christian faith has come about as the result of various theories of the end time that not only say Jesus will return but predict his every movement. In some ways, the hole in the sky where Jesus was is filled for some by the certainty they believe they have found in their own apocalyptic scheme. Many who have been wounded or put off by such schemes resolve to lay aside any notion of Jesus' return.

This might be the Sunday to give a survey of the various apocalyptic options and their implications. I suspect that one of the strengths of the mainline experience may not be that it has either given lip service to the end time or sought to completely lay it aside. Can we do this and remain faithful in any sense to Luke's understanding as well as the vision of the Christian scripture?

Easter 7
Acts 1:6-14
1 Peter 4:12-14; 5:6-11
John 17:1-11
by Wayne Brouwer

Invisible link

Now and again, one of my students will come into class and I'll greet her or him but get no response. Sometimes I'll even walk up to the student when she sits down and make my presence obvious. Then she will look up startled, pull back her hood, and yank the buds out of her ears or turn down her iPod so that she re-engages the world in which I exist. When her recorded music was shouted in her ears, she became deaf to this world and alive to another.

In a sense, that is what each of today's lectionary passages wants to have happen in the Christian's life. Only when we are uniquely and overwhelmingly connected to the music of eternity, and live in the reality of God's glory, can we keep our purpose and identity true (Acts 1), avoid the wiles of the devil (1 Peter 4-5), and nurture a passion that shines with God's own glory (John 17).

Acts 1:6-14

The existence of the Christian church is rooted in several theological declarations. First, we believe that there is a God who created this world and uniquely fashioned our human race with attributes that reflect its maker. Second, through human willfulness the world lost its pristine vitality and is now caught up in a civil war against its Creator. Third, by intruding directly into human affairs for the sake of reclaiming and restoring the world, the Creator began a mission of redemption and renewal through the nation of Israel, shaped by the Suzerain-Vassal covenant formed at Mount Sinai and positioned at the crossroads of global societies as a witness to all peoples. Fourth, because of the inadequacy of this method of operations as the human race expanded rapidly, the Creator revised the divine missional strategy, and interrupted human history again in the person of Jesus, who embodied the divine essence, taught the divine will, and through whose death and resurrection established a new understanding of eschatological hope. Fifth, the coming of this messianic age was foretold by the prophets of Israel who called it the "Day of the Lord" and identified its three major aspects: divine judgment on the sins of all nations (including Israel), the sparing of a remnant from Israel who would be the restored seed community of a new global divine initiative, and the coming of the eschatological messianic age in which righteousness and justice would renew both human society and the natural order so that people could again live out their intended purposes and destinies. Sixth, Jesus split this "Day of the Lord" in two bringing the beginnings of its eternal blessings while withholding the full impact of divine judgment for a time. Seventh, the Christian church is God's new agent for global missional recovery and restoration for the human race.

Each of these themes is implied or explicit in the first two chapters of the book of the Acts of the Apostles. God and sin and the divine mission are all part of the fabric, while Israel's role in the divine mission, along with the changing strategies, is declared openly. Jesus is at the center of all these things, but the unique divine intrusion he brought into the human race is now being withdrawn, and the church must become the ongoing embodiment of Jesus' life and teachings so that it may live out the divine mission until the remainder of the "Day of the Lord" arrives when Jesus returns.

This is seen in the few, but packed, verses of today's lectionary reading. First, Jesus' disciples are beside themselves with new hope and confidence, since their rabbi has become a death-defeating powerhouse.

They see the future in a limited (mis)understanding of all the promises of the prophets — Israel restored, victorious over the nations, and re-established as the most glorious and wealthy society on earth. Jesus, however, reads history in a new way, marking the change of divine mission strategy from that tied to the geography of Palestine through Israel's national witness to the dispersion of the church among the nations of the earth.

Second, in Jesus' ascension there is a twofold word of promise. On the one hand, Jesus' disappearance is a vote of confidence in his disciples. He is affirming that the work he has begun will be in good hands when left with them. In fact, in the early church there was a parabolic teaching that said when Jesus returned to heaven, amid the triumphant praise of the angels, Gabriel asked his master what contingency plan Jesus had left on earth. "Oh," said Jesus, "I've spent a little time with some fishermen and social misfits and housewives, and they will take care of things now."

Gabriel was stunned. "That's not very encouraging," he said. "You were only with them for three years and most of them ran out on you when things turned tough. Now you leave the whole mission of God in their hands? I don't get it. What's the backup plan?"

But the early church knew Jesus' response. He shook his head slowly and with a smile, said, "There is no backup plan. They won't fail. They're my people, and I trust them. I trust them."

On the other hand, Jesus' ascension is stage-managed by "two men dressed in white" who announce the end already at the beginning, by promising the Lord's planned return. In this way, Luke communicates the message that the church lives under eschatological urgency. There is a job to be done: witnessing about Jesus. But those who are going to make testimony are on the clock, and the hours are ticking away. Furthermore, if Jesus is the "Day of the Lord," and his first coming inaugurated the blessings of the messianic age, his second coming will finalize the judgments of God on all that is evil and sinful. Therefore, the work to be done is critical in changing the eternal outcomes for all who live in these times.

Third, Luke spends a little time again on his grand theme of the fellowship of the worshiping community. In his gospel, Luke began with a scene of worship in the temple (Luke 1) and ended with a similar incident (Luke 24). Moreover, the early chapters of the gospel were filled with songs and prayers (Zechariah, Mary, the angels, Simeon). Now again, Luke introduces the great work of Jesus through the church by the power of the Holy Spirit with a scene of worshiping fellowship and prayer. What is interesting this time is that it does not take place in the temple. For good reason, of course — from this time forward the strategy of the mission of God changes. No longer is the divine intent to bring nations to Israel and the temple to view the glory of the creator there. Instead, the worshiping fellowship will be dispersed among the nations of the world and people will find God in these pockets of prayer and praise called the church.

Luke certainly wants to keep the focus on the events in this dimension. But it is also wonderful to use his ascension story to imagine what happened in heaven that day. Can you see the angels welcoming back their Creator who has become their ward under protection? Can you imagine the tear in the eye of the Father as the Son returns in humble triumph after changing the course of human history, as well as sealing the blessed fate of the stars and galaxies? Can you feel the resonant praise of celestial choirs in the celebration that reverberated to the far reaches of the expanding universe? Can you sense the awe of the archangel Michael as he touched the scars in the human flesh that was now forever wedded to the Son's divine nature? Chuck Girard's great song "Hear The Angels Sing" seems to fit the atmosphere of the occasion.

1 Peter 4:12-14; 5:6-11

Peter was probably aware of the great suffering that was about to unfold as the ominous winds of Nero's power whipped the Roman world. While he begins writing in powerful terms of the great salvation recently brought to humankind through Jesus, and irreversibly guaranteed, by way of Jesus' resurrection and ascension, for those who believe (1 Peter 1:3-12), he quickly moves on to an extended exhortation to holy living, because these believers in Jesus are God's special people (1 Peter 1:13—2:10), who follow in the footsteps of Jesus (1 Peter 2:11—3:12), and must face, with their master, the sufferings that will fall on all his disciples in these challenging times (1 Peter 3:12—4:19). The tone of Peter's letter is troubled. There is an ominous pall of suffering that clouds every perspective. Jesus suffered. You will suffer, if you are faithful. You must follow Jesus in and through suffering. New trials and greater suffering are coming.

Yet through the murky shrieks and dark valleys, Peter never loses confidence in God's sovereignty or care. This is the constant underlying theme. Especially in the verses of today's lectionary reading, Peter declares that God is judge of evil, faithful creator, and the chief shepherd who will soon bring untarnishing crowns of glory for those who remain true.

This is an important message, particularly in light of the warnings Peter issues about the wiles of the devil. Persistence often conquers resistance, especially as cunning as the evil one can be. Offering pleasures that appear harmless, they are usually ultimately deadly. Following the path of least resistance, as one person put it, is what makes people and rivers crooked.

We need to learn resistance in many ways in order to survive in life. When two Russian cosmonauts returned to earth in 1982 after 211 days in space, they suffered from dizziness, high pulse rates, and heart palpitations. They couldn't walk for a week. A month later they were still undergoing therapy for atrophied muscles and weakened hearts. In the zero gravity of outer space, their muscles had begun to waste away. Scientists had to design "resistance suits" to counteract the unseen predator. Only with resistance applied against the muscles of the body could they remain strong.

Ben Weir, in his book, *Hostage Bound, Hostage Free* (Westminster, 1987), translated this into spiritual terms. He documented the inner resistance that saved his life. During his many months of captivity in Beirut there was a constant nagging to give in to depression and give up to despair. Although his situation was excessive, far beyond that which we normally face, it condensed into eighteen months the wasting that can happen in any spirit over the years. Charles Darwin, who grew up in a strong Presbyterian home, said, in his later years, that he never rejected the Christian faith; instead, he said, it gradually lost its importance to him as he ceased to use it — no resistance, no resurgence — no test, no tensile — no effort, no energy.

Someone told me recently of a young man who was buying his own clothes in preparation for college. He asked a sales clerk what the tag meant when it said "Shrink Resistant." The clerk replied, "Even though that shirt doesn't want to shrink, it will!"

Most of us could wear a label like that on our souls. Only the disciplines of faith cause it to fall off as our resistance to the devil grows.

John 17:1-11

In many respects, this chapter can more appropriately be called "The Lord's Prayer" than the other familiar lines that usually go by that name. Here, Jesus bares his soul before his Father and his disciples in a truly powerful and passionate expression of love and commitment. There are two overarching themes throughout the prayer: unity and mission. Both of these come together in the word Jesus repeatedly uses: glory. The Father lives in splendid glory from before all time. Jesus shares the Father's glory. Jesus came to earth on a mission of revealing the Father's glory in the world darkened by sin, particularly to his disciples. Now Jesus is sending his disciples out to continue that mission and only the glory of God can bind them together and to heaven's purpose.

They will need Jesus' prayers; though their cause is great, the pitfalls are plentiful. Fred Craddock, retired professor of homiletics at Emory University, says we all have this glorious image of ourselves when we first stand up and confess Jesus Christ, like Jesus' own disciples. Craddock says that it is as if we have been given a brand-new starched and stiff $1,000 bill. We take it to Jesus and shout, "Here! Here's my life! Here's my wealth! Here's all of my being! Take me, Jesus! I give myself to you!"

Jesus takes our bright and shiny and crinkly $1,000 bill. But then he hands it back to us. "Go to the bank," he says. "Cash it in for nickels and dimes."

When we do that, coming home with buckets and baskets and wheelbarrows of coins, he says to us, "Now give me fifteen cents a day for the rest of your life."

All excited, we start out with a flourish. A nickel and a dime set aside each morning. But there are always so many other things to buy, so many other toys to play with, and soon the nickels and dimes are gone. So is our faith. And so is our uncompromising devotion. Like the beggars on the street, we walk around with limp hands and feeble hearts.

It's easy to love your spouse on the day of your wedding. It's easy to make commitments for a lifetime in the heat of passion. It's easy to soar on a blazing glory star of faith when you join the church. But the world around says: "You'll never make it. You'll never keep your vows. You'll never last."

Jesus knew this about the twelve he had gathered as his own. He also knows it about us and that is why John included this prayer in his gospel. We have to know how hard Jesus is wrestling for us and our passions. When Jesus asks us for a slow and steady devotion rather than a martyr's burst of passion, we often die inch by inch, a nickel and a dime at a time.

One mother tells this story about her son. He earned a little spending money every winter by shoveling snow from people's driveways. He walks up and down their street. One morning, after a heavy snowfall, he seemed awfully slow in leaving the house. She asked him if there was anything wrong. "No," he said, "I'm just waiting until people get started. I get most of my jobs from people who want to quit halfway through."

Jesus wants to make sure his disciples are going for the goal. He pleads with the Father that they won't drop out of the race. Jesus knows they will be knocked down by their own pride and passions now and again and sometimes by the storms of others. But Jesus begs for the power of God to get them up and running again, a nickel and dime each morning, and heading for the finish line of God's glory.

How does that happen? In a sense, Jesus wants to inspire them with the kind of "magnificent obsession" that author Lloyd Douglas wrote about in his novel of that name. The book is about a fellow named Robert Merrick. He's young. He's rich. He's drunk. Life is a game for him, a game of using people and tossing them aside. A game of playing with his toys in his self-centered world.

Then it happens: He's out on his yacht, the wind catches the sail and throws the boom at him, he falls into the water, unconscious, and is rescued, barely alive. At the same moment, a world-famous doctor, dedicated, devoted, a saver of lives, drowns in a freak accident just down the beach. Young Merrick lies in the hospital. His eyes are closed and everybody thinks he's unconscious. Two nurses stand over him and one shakes her head.

"What a tragedy..." she says. "A great man who saves lives [is] lost, and this fellow, who never did any good for anybody, [is] saved!"

Merrick knows it's true. He's alive but he's never really lived. He was pulled from the water but for no good reason. In that moment, in that instant of judgment, Merrick gains his "magnificent obsession." He'll go to university. He'll get a degree in medicine. He'll take the doctor's place. He'll save lives and begin to truly live himself.

A magnificent obsession! A purpose for which to live and a cause for which to die. That's the atmosphere that pervades Jesus' prayer. My Father! The glory of God! Jesus' magnificent obsession carries him and those who are his on from glory to glory (2 Corinthians 3:18).

Application

Richard Mouw, in his book, *Calvinism in the Las Vegas Airport*, mentions a conversation with an immigrant from eastern Europe. He had asked her where she was from, and she told him all about her former community, family, and especially her grandmother. When she turned the tables and asked him where *he* was from, he said, "Oh, a suburb of Los Angeles." But that meant nothing to her.

"No!" she said. "Where are you *from*? Who was your grandmother?" She meant to get at the culture that made him the person he was today.

So with these lectionary passages. The goal is to get our people to know who they are, *whose* they are, and to claim that identity as their primary point of reference in all things.

An Alternative Application

Acts 1:6-14. If you did not yet celebrate Jesus' ascension, today is the day to make use of Acts 1 and talk about Jesus' finished work, his coronation day in heaven, and the trust he bestows on his church as we carry on with the transforming mission of God's evangelistic grace.

About the Authors

Wayne Brouwer teaches Religion, Theology, and Ministry Studies at both Hope College and Western Theological Seminary in Holland, Michigan. He holds degrees from Dordt College (A.B.), Calvin Theological Seminary (M.Div., Th.M.), and McMaster University (M.A., Ph.D.), and spent three decades as a pastor and international missionary teacher. Along with hundreds of published articles, Wayne Brouwer has authored thirteen books, including *Covenant Documents: Reading the Bible Again for the First Time* (Cognella), *The Literary Development of John 13-17: A Chiastic Reading* (SBL), and *Being a Believer in an Unbelieving World* (Hendrickson).

Timothy B. Cargal currently serves as Associate for Preparation for Ministry with the General Assembly of the Presbyterian Church (USA). For some twenty years he combined pastoral ministry with teaching biblical studies in universities and seminaries. He is the author of two books, including *Hearing a Film, Seeing a Sermon: Preaching and Popular Movies* (Westminster John Knox Press), and has contributed to several other books, study bibles, dictionaries, and journals in the areas of New Testament studies and preaching. He holds a Ph.D. in Religious Studies from Vanderbilt University.

David Kalas is the pastor of First United Methodist Church in Green Bay, Wisconsin. Before moving to Green Bay, he pastored churches in Whitewater, Wisconsin; Appleton, Wisconsin; and Hurt, Virginia. He also led youth ministries in Cleveland, Ohio, and Richmond, Virginia. David earned his undergraduate degree from the University of Virginia in Charlottesville and his Master of Divinity degree from Union Theological Seminary in Richmond, Virginia. He has also done coursework at Pittsburgh Theological Seminary and Asbury Theological Seminary.

In addition to the present volume, David has also contributed to other preaching resources published by CSS, is a regular contributor to *Emphasis: A Lectionary Preaching Journal* (CSS Publishing Company, Inc.), and has also written curriculum materials for the United Methodist Publishing House. David and his wife, Karen, have been married nearly 30 years and have three daughters, Angela, Lydia, and Susanna.

The late **R. Craig MacCreary** was pastor of South Congregational Church, United Church of Christ in Newport, New Hampshire. He held pastorates in Pennsylvania, West Virginia, and Massachusetts. He earned degrees from Elon University (B.A.), Lancaster Theological Seminary (M. Div.), and Hartford Seminary (D. Min.). His work appeared in *Colleague*, *Pulpit Digest*, and *The United Church News*. He was a guest on National Public Radio and was a contributor to *Candles in the Dark: Preaching and Poetry in Times of Crises*, edited by James Randolph.

Mark Molldrem has served as a pastor in the Evangelical Lutheran Church in America for 37 years. He has had parishes in Cobb/Edmund, Wisconsin; Beaver Dam, Wisconsin; Mondovi/Modena, Wisconsin; and Saginaw, Michigan. Currently he is Senior Pastor at First Lutheran Church in Beaver Dam, Wisconsin. Molldrem has written previously for CSS. He has authored numerous articles in various national magazines and journals. He received his Master of Divinity and also his Doctor of Ministry degrees from Luther Theological Seminary, St. Paul, Minnesota. He is very involved in his community, supporting People Against a Violent Environment (domestic violence) and developing community leadership through the Chamber of Commerce. Throughout the years, he has enjoyed art glass, martial arts, landscaping, preaching and teaching in the Lutheran Church in Liberia (West Africa), playing with his grandchildren, and vacationing with his wife, Shirley, with whom he has raised two children.

William H. Shepherd is an author, teacher, biblical scholar, and Episcopal priest who currently serves as an Interim Ministry Specialist in the Diocese of Connecticut. In addition to 19 years of experience in parish ministry, he has taught preaching and biblical studies at Candler School of Theology, Virginia Theological Seminary, George Mercer Memorial School of Theology, and Immaculate Conception Seminary. Shepherd's writing has appeared in *Christian Century*, *Anglican Theological Review*, *Emphasis: A Preaching Journal for the Parish Pastor*, and several other publications. He is a graduate of the University of Georgia, Yale Divinity School, and received his Ph.D. in New Testament studies from Emory University.